The Index
of Leading
Cultural Indicators

*Facts and Figures on the
State of American Society*

William J. Bennett

A Touchstone Book
Published by SIMON & SCHUSTER
New York   London   Toronto   Sydney   Tokyo   Singapore

TOUCHSTONE
Rockefeller Center
1230 Avenue of the Americas
New York, New York 10020

TOUCHSTONE and colophon are registered trademarks of
Simon & Schuster Inc.

Designed by Irving Perkins Associates
Manufactured in the United States of America
4   6   8   10   9   7   5
Library of Congress Cataloging-in-Publication Data is available.

ISBN: 0-671-88326-7

Contents

Introduction

The Index of Leading Cultural Indicators grew out of a report by the same name I released in March 1993. The concept for both the original report and this book originated in the economic world. In the early 1960s, the U.S. Bureau of the Census, responding to the economic needs of the nation, began publishing key indicators that provided an assessment of the overall condition of the American economy. Known as the Index of Leading Economic Indicators, these 11 indicators, taken together, represent the best means we now have of interpreting current business developments and predicting future economic trends.

The Index of Leading Cultural Indicators attempts to bring a similar kind of empirical analysis to cultural issues. It is an assessment of the moral, social, and behavioral condition of modern American society. This idea may seem fairly novel, but it is not new to history. During the early stages of nineteenth-century industrialization, historian Thomas Carlyle spoke about the "condition of England question." For Carlyle, the answer to the "condition of England question" lay not in "figures of arithmetic," but in the realm of behavior, habits, beliefs, and mores—matters that in our time often travel under the banner of "values."

The Index of Leading Cultural Indicators is the most comprehensive statistical portrait available of behavioral trends over the last 30 years. It consists of five chapters: Crime; Family and Children; Youth Pathologies and Behavior; Education; Popular Culture and Religion; along with appendices on social spending and various economic indicators. This book includes social indicators that provide statistical and numerical breakdowns (beginning in 1960 and

done in five-year increments, whenever data is available); charts
and graphs; an extensive factual analysis of our current cultural
condition; and commentaries that provide perspective on, and
interpretation of, the raw data. The purpose, then, is to provide an
empirical assessment of the "condition of America question." And
according to the findings in this book, in many ways the condition
of America is not good.

Over the past three decades we have experienced substantial
social regression. Today the forces of social decomposition are challenging—and in some instances, overtaking—the forces of social
composition. And when decomposition takes hold, it exacts an
enormous human cost. *Unless these exploding social pathologies are reversed,
they will lead to the decline and perhaps even to the fall of the American republic.*

Since 1960, population has increased 41 percent; the Gross
Domestic Product has nearly tripled; and total levels of spending
by all levels of government (measured in constant 1990 dollars)
have risen from $143.73 billion to $787.0 billion—more than a
five-fold increase. Inflation-adjusted spending on welfare has
increased 630 percent and inflation-adjusted spending on education has increased more than 200 percent. The United States has
the strongest economy in the world, a healthy entrepreneurial
spirit, a still-healthy work ethic, and a generous attitude—good
signs all.

But during the same 30-year period there has been more than a
500 percent increase in violent crime; more than a 400 percent
increase in illegitimate births; a tripling of the percentage of children living in single-parent homes; a tripling in the teenage suicide rate; a doubling in the divorce rate; and a drop of almost 75
points in SAT scores. Modern-day social pathologies have gotten
worse. They seem impervious to government spending on their
alleviation, even very large amounts of spending.

Although the Great Society experienced some successes, there is
a growing body of evidence that indicates its remedies have, in
many cases, reached their limits. Many of the most serious behavioral problems we now face (particularly among our young) are
remarkably resistant to government cures. How intelligently and
honestly we address these problems is the critical social policy
question of the decade.

In the summer of 1990 a special commission of prominent political, medical, education, and business leaders issued a report on the health of America's teenagers, titled *Code Blue*. They wrote that "never before has one generation of American teenagers been less healthy, less cared for, or less prepared for life than their parents were at the same age." According to the commission, the explanation for teenagers' deteriorating condition lies with their behavior and not (as was the case in the past) with physical illness.

A disturbing and telling sign of the declining condition among the young is evident in an on-going teacher survey. Over the years teachers have been asked to identify the top problems in America's public schools. In 1940, teachers identified talking out of turn; chewing gum; making noise; running in the halls; cutting in line; dress code infractions; and littering. When asked the same question in 1990, teachers identified drug abuse; alcohol abuse; pregnancy; suicide; rape; robbery; and assault.

This palpable cultural decline is the manifestation of a marked shift in the public's beliefs, attitudes, and priorities. Social scientist James Q. Wilson writes that "the powers exercised by the institutions of social control have been constrained and people, especially young people, have embraced an ethos that values self-expression over self-control." According to pollster Daniel Yankelovich, our society now places less value than before on what we owe others as a matter of moral obligation; less value on sacrifice as a moral good; less value on social conformity, respectability, and observing the rules; and less value on correctness and restraint in matters of physical pleasure and sexuality. Higher value is now placed on things like self-expression, individualism, self-realization, and personal choice.

Some of our greatest modern-day writers have spoken eloquently on these matters. The novelist Walker Percy was asked what issue most concerned him about the future of our nation. Percy answered, "Probably the fear of seeing America, with all its great strength and beauty and freedom...gradually subside into decay through default and be defeated, not by the Communist movement, demonstrably a bankrupt system, but from within by weariness, boredom, cynicism, greed and in the end helplessness before its great problems." Nobel Prize–winning author Aleksandr

Solzhenitsyn, in a recent speech, said, "The West . . . has been undergoing an erosion and obscuring of high moral and ethical ideas. The spiritual axis of life has grown dim." And novelist John Updike has put it this way: "The fact that, compared to the inhabitants of Africa and Russia, we still live well, cannot ease the pain of feeling we no longer live nobly."

Treatises have been written on why this has occurred, on why we have allowed this to occur. The hard truth is that in a free society the ultimate responsibility rests with the people themselves. It is our beliefs, our behavior, and our philosophy that have in many instances changed for the worse. Our injury is self-inflicted; the good news is that what has been self-inflicted can be self-corrected.

I believe that there are some things that politics in general, and government in particular, can do to encourage cultural renewal. First, government should heed the old injunction, "Do no harm." Over the years the government has often done unintended harm to many of the people it was trying to help. There are intrinsic flaws in some programs. This is particularly, though by no means exclusively, true of programs aimed at assisting the underclass. Before writing social policy we should ask some basic questions, such as: What kind of behavior will this legislation encourage or discourage? Will this legislation undermine families? Will it encourage individual responsibility or dependency? Will it provide effective assistance and succor to those in need, or will assistance be diverted to massive bureaucracies? And, is this the kind of activity that government *ought* to be involved in? These questions may seem obvious, but too often they have been ignored.

Second, political leaders can help shape social attitudes through public discourse and through social legislation. One of the best recent examples of how laws can give voice to our moral beliefs is the civil rights legislation of the 1950s and 1960s. Here was statecraft as soulcraft. We should do more of it.

Third, a reform-minded and thoughtful legislative social agenda should include:

❏ A more effective and tough-minded criminal justice system, including more prisons, judges, and prosecutors; a reform of the juvenile criminal justice system (including trying as adults juveniles who commit certain violent crimes); increased attention to victims' rights and roles in the criminal justice process; reform of parole; enactment of "truth in sentencing" guidelines (ensuring that convicted criminals serve, at minimum, half their sentence); alternative forms of punishment, such as boot camps; community-based policing; and an integrated anti-drug strategy;

❏ A radical reform of education through national standards, merit pay, alternative certification, a core curriculum, and allowing parents to choose the public, private, or religious schools to which they send their children;

❏ A reversal of the destructive incentives of the welfare system by ending payments at a certain date; by reducing the economic penalties on marriage for single mothers; and by requiring welfare mothers with older children to contribute community service in exchange for benefits received;

❏ Removal of the economic barriers that keep the underclass in poverty by providing tax incentives for business to locate in urban enterprise zones, tenant ownership, and investment in low-income housing;

❏ Support for families by increasing the federal personal income tax dependent exemption;

❏ Removal of major obstacles to adoption and increasing the number of residential schools, congregate care facilities, and orphanages for abandoned and abused children;

❏ Improvement in efforts to collect child-support payments (for example, by requiring parents to report child-support obligations to the IRS, which can deduct delinquent payments from tax refunds);

❏ Identification of the father of every child, by having states ensure that a document exists at birth to identify the name and Social Security number of both parents; and

❏ Insisting that fathers take responsibility for their children through support of community organizations and programs (like Charles Ballard's National Institute for Responsible Fatherhood) that are dedicated to seeing to it that fathers legitimize their children, attend school, and find gainful employment.

This legislative agenda would have a positive impact. *But we must look beyond government.* In general we should temper our expectations—particularly our short-term expectations—of government. The last quarter-century has taught politicians a hard and humbling lesson: there are real limits to what the state can do, particularly when it comes to imparting virtue and forming character. Never before has the reach of government been greater or its purse larger—and never before have our social pathologies been worse. Samuel Johnson put it well: "How small, of all that human hearts endure,/That part which laws or kings can cause or cure!"

Our social and civic institutions—families, churches, schools, neighborhoods, and civic associations—have traditionally taken on the responsibility for providing our children with love and order; discipline and self-control; compassion and tolerance; civility and respect for legitimate authority; fidelity and honesty. These responsibilities, replicated through the generations, are among the constitutive acts of civilization. When these institutions fail, others may need to step in. But government, even at its best, can never be more than an auxiliary in the development of a free people's moral disposition and character.

The social regression of the last 30 years is due in large part to the enfeebled state of our social institutions and their failure to carry out a critical and time-honored task: the moral education of the young. We desperately need to recover a sense of the fundamental purpose of education, which is to engage in the architecture of souls. When a self-governing society ignores this responsibility, then, as this book demonstrates, it does so at its peril.

William J. Bennett
January 1994

Acknowledgment

I wish to thank the Heritage Foundation, and especially its president, Edwin J. Feulner, Jr., and its executive vice president, Phillip N. Truluck, for their encouragement, assistance, and cooperation in the preparation and publication of the original *Index of Leading Cultural Indicators*, the report that was the inspiration for this book.

The Index
of Leading
Cultural Indicators

Chapter 1

Crime

Total Crimes

❏ *Since 1960, total crimes have increased by more than 300 percent.*

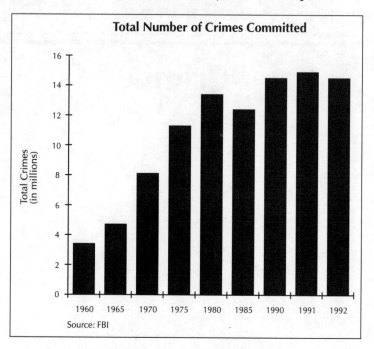

Total Number of Crimes Committed

Source: FBI

Total Number of Crimes Committed

Year	Total Crimes	Total Crime Rate (per 10,000)
1960	3,384,200	188.7
1965	4,739,400	249.9
1970	8,098,000	398.5
1975	11,292,400	459.9
1980	13,408,300	595.0
1985	12,431,400	520.5
1990	14,475,600	582.0
1991	14,872,900	589.8
1992	14,438,191	566.0

Source: FBI

Factual Overview: Total Crime

❑ In 1992, there were more than 14 million crimes committed in the United States.[1]

❑ In 1992, the average total crimes per 100,000 population in the United States was 5,660. The ten states with the highest rates of total crime are as follows:[2]

Total Crime **Top Ten States: 1992**	
State	Crimes per 100,000
Florida	8,358
Texas	7,057
Arizona	7,028
California	6,679
Louisiana	6,546
New Mexico	6,434
Georgia	6,405
Maryland	6,225
Nevada	6,204
Washington	6,173

Source: FBI

❑ Poor households suffer the highest victimization rates for property and personal crimes.[3]

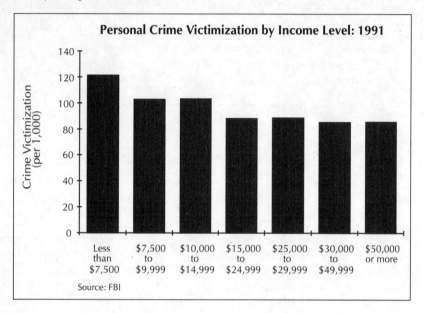

Personal Crime Victimization by Income Level: 1991

Crime Victimization (per 1,000)

Less than $7,500	
$7,500 to $9,999	
$10,000 to $14,999	
$15,000 to $24,999	
$25,000 to $29,999	
$30,000 to $49,999	
$50,000 or more	

Source: FBI

❑ Ninety-nine percent of Americans will be victims of theft at least once in their lives. Eighty-seven percent will have property stolen three or more times.[4]

Commentary on Crime

❑ "Among the many objects to which a wise and free people find it necessary to direct their attention, that of providing for their *safety* seems to be the first."[5]

—JOHN JAY
Federalist No. 3, 1787

❑ "No society will long remain open and attached to peaceable politics and the decent and controlled use of public force if fear for personal safety is the ordinary experience of large numbers."[6]

—ALEXANDER BICKEL
Yale University

❏ "There is an expectation of crime in our lives. We are in danger of becoming captive to that expectation, and to the new tolerance to criminal behavior, not only in regard to violent crime. A number of years ago there began to appear, in the windows of automobiles parked on the streets of American cities, signs which read: 'No radio.' Rather than express outrage, or even annoyance at the possibility of a car break-in, people tried to communicate with the potential thief in conciliatory terms. The translation of 'no radio' is: 'Please break into someone else's car, there's nothing in mine.' These 'no radio' signs are flags of urban surrender. They are hand-written capitulations. Instead of 'no radio,' we need new signs that say 'no surrender.'"[7]

—RAYMOND KELLY
Former New York City
Police Commissioner

❏ "The natural dynamic of the marketplace cannot assert itself when a local economy is regulated by crime. . . . Crime is the ultimate tax on enterprise."[8]

—JAMES K. STEWART
Former Director of the National
Institute of Justice

❏ "During the 1960s, one neighborhood in San Francisco had the lowest income, the highest unemployment rate, the highest proportion of families with incomes under $4,000 a year, the least educational attainment, the highest tuberculosis rate, and the highest proportion of substandard housing. . . . That neighborhood was called Chinatown. Yet in 1965, there were only five persons of Chinese ancestry committed to prison in the entire state of California."[9]

—JAMES Q. WILSON and
RICHARD HERRNSTEIN
University of California,
Los Angeles
Harvard University

Violent Crimes

❏ **While population has increased only 41 percent since 1960, the number of violent crimes* has increased more than 550 percent.**

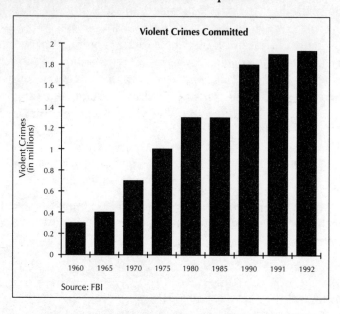

Violent Crimes Committed

Source: FBI

Year	Violent Crimes	Violent Crime Rates (per 10,000)
1960	288,460	16.1
1965	387,390	20.0
1970	738,820	36.4
1975	1,039,710	48.8
1980	1,344,520	59.7
1985	1,273,280	53.3
1990	1,820,130	73.2
1991	1,911,770	75.8
1992	1,932,274	75.8

Source: FBI

* "Violent crimes" include murders, rapes, robberies, and aggravated assaults.

Factual Overview: Violent Crime Increase

❏ Eight out of every 10 Americans can expect to be the victim of violent crime at least once in their lives.[10]

❏ The rate of violent crime in the United States is worse than in any other industrialized country. The United States' homicide rate is more than five times that of Europe, and four times that of Canada, Australia, or New Zealand. In addition, the rate at which rapes occur in the United States is nearly seven times higher than it is in Europe.[11]

❏ Violent crimes increased about 50 percent between 1985 and 1992. In 1992, there were 23,760 murders, 109,062 forcible rapes, 672,478 acts of robbery, and 1.1 million cases of aggravated assault.[12]

❏ Since 1990, more than 90,000 people have been murdered, about twice as many Americans than were killed in the Vietnam War.[13]

❏ In 1943 in New York City, there were 44 homicides by gunshot. In 1991 there were 1,499 homicides by gunshot in New York City.[14]

Factual Overview: Police Deployment

❏ In the 1950s there were 3.2 police in urban America for every violent felony committed. Now the reverse is true: there are 3.2 crimes per police officer. In most big cities, the problem is even worse—6.9 violent felonies per police officer in Boston, 6.5 in New York and Chicago, and 10 in Los Angeles, Atlanta, and Newark.[15]

❏ Estimates are that a 20 percent increase in the police forces of the 222 local police departments that in 1990 served populations of 100,000 or more would cost about $1 billion a year. The social benefits would almost certainly exceed the costs, as would be evident in reduced criminal victimization, revitalized local economies, and enhanced respect for government.[16]

❏ From 1979 to 1990, total per capita spending by all levels of government on justice system activities rose 35 percent, with a 31 percent increase for courts, 55 percent for prosecutors, and 99 percent for corrections. Spending for police, however, rose only 6 percent.[17]

❏ In our nation's largest cities, the number of police officers deployed on the street at any given time is typically less than one for every several thousand city residents. For example, Chicago has one officer patrolling the streets for every 3,500 residents; in Atlanta, one officer per 4,000 residents; in New York, one officer per 4,200 residents; and in San Francisco, one police officer for each 6,200 residents.[18]

Factual Overview: Guns

❏ In 1991, Americans owned 201.8 million firearms—66.7 million handguns, 72.7 million rifles, and 62.4 million shotguns.[19]

❏ In 1991, 66.3 percent of all murders were firearm-related, with 53.1 percent involving handguns, and 3.4 percent involving rifles. About 40 percent of all robberies and 24 percent of all aggravated assaults involved a firearm.[20]

❏ From 1960 to 1980, the population of the United States increased by 26 percent while the homicide rate due to guns increased 160 percent.[21]

❏ Of the guns obtained by violent criminals, 93 percent are not obtained through the lawful purchase and sale transactions that are the object of most gun control legislation.[22]

❏ Armed citizens defend their lives or property with firearms against criminals approximately 1 million times a year. In 98 percent of these instances, the citizen merely brandishes the weapon or fires a warning shot. Only in 2 percent of the cases do citizens actually shoot their assailants. In defending themselves with their firearms, armed citizens kill 2,000 to 3,000 criminals each year—three times the number killed by police.[23]

Factual Overview: Victimization

❏ Every year 5 million people are victims of violent crimes—murder, rape, robbery, or assault. Nineteen million Americans are victims of property crimes—arson, burglary, and larceny-theft.[24]

❏ From 1960 to 1991, the rate of homicide deaths among children under the age of 19 has more than quadrupled.[25]

❏ In 1991, in Los Angeles, there was a greater chance that a citizen would die from a bullet wound than from a traffic accident. In 1991, 1,554 people were killed by gunfire, while 1,215 died in traffic accidents.[26]

❏ Teenagers are two and one-half times more likely to be victims of violent crimes than those over age 20.[27]

❏ The cities with the highest rates of murders, rapes, and robberies are:[28]

Cities (population over 250,000) with Highest Rates of Murders, Rapes, and Robberies: 1991 (per 100,000)					
Murders		Rapes		Robberies	
Washington	76	Cleveland	166	Newark	1,942
Detroit	57	Atlanta	153	Miami	1,890
St. Louis	57	Birmingham	133	Baltimore	1,623
New Orleans	55	Cincinnati	131	Atlanta	1,417
Birmingham	49	Kansas City	128	Chicago	1,356
Source: FBI					

Factual Overview: Violent Criminals

❏ Single men comprise 13 percent of the total population, yet they account for 40 percent of all criminal offenders and commit 90 percent of all violent crimes.[29]

❏ According to studies, less than 10 percent of all criminals commit about two-thirds of all crimes.[30]

❏ The Bureau of Alcohol, Tobacco and Firearms estimates that the average armed career criminal commits three crimes per week.[31]

Factual Overview: Violent Crime by Race

❑ Whites make up about 80 percent of the population, and account for about 54 percent of all violent criminal offenders.[32]

❑ Blacks make up about 12 percent of the population, and account for about 45 percent of all violent criminal offenders.[33]

❑ A young black man living in Harlem is less likely to live until the age of 40 than a young man in Bangladesh.[34]

❑ While the murder rate for white males, white females, and black females ages 10 to 17 has remained relatively stable during the past 15 years, the murder rate for black males ages 10 to 17 has more than doubled.[35]

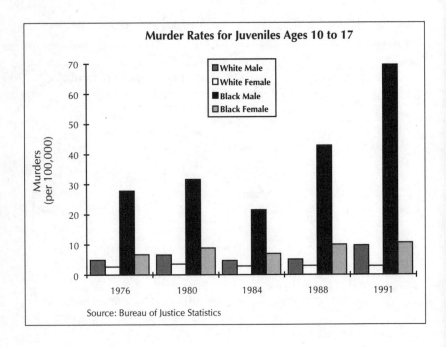

Murder Rates for Juveniles Ages 10 to 17

Source: Bureau of Justice Statistics

❑ The vast majority of violent crimes against blacks were committed by other blacks. For murders in 1990 in which there was a single offender and a single victim (about 53 percent of murders known to police), 93 percent of the black murder victims were murdered by a black offender. In 1990, 83.9 percent of black violent crime victims reported that the offender was also black. White offenders accounted for 8.9 percent of violent crimes against blacks in 1990.[36]

❏ Between 1976 and 1991, the homicide victimization rate among white youth remained flat at about 2 to 3 murders per 100,000. In contrast, between 1976 and 1986, the homicide victimization rate among African-American youth fluctuated between 7 and 10 murders per 100,000, then increased steadily to about 14 in 1988 and 20 in 1991. Homicide is now far and away the leading cause of death among African-American teenagers.[37]

Commentary on Violent Crime

❏ "In 1929 in Chicago during Prohibition, four gangsters killed seven gangsters on February 14. The nation was shocked. The event became legend. It merits not one but two entries in the World Book Encyclopedia. I leave it to others to judge, but it would appear that the society in the 1920s was simply not willing to put up with this degree of deviancy. In the end, the Constitution was amended, and Prohibition, which lay behind so much gangster violence, ended."[38]

—DANIEL PATRICK MOYNIHAN
United States Senator

❏ "The deviant—criminals who assault, rape, rob, murder and deal drugs—ruin their neighborhoods by making local business, development and economic transformation impossible. Where the deviant rule, conservatives can forget about the magic of enterprise zones and liberals can forget about the promise of new social welfare measures."[39]

—JOHN J. DIIULIO, JR.
Princeton University

❏ "[There is a] nearly invisible relationship between unemployment and crime rates. Charting homicide since 1900 reveals two peaks. The first is in 1933. This represents the crest of a wave that began in 1905, continued through the prosperous '20s and then began to *decline* in 1934 as the Great Depression was deepening. Between 1933 and 1940, the murder rate dropped nearly 40 percent. Property crimes reveal a similar pattern."[40]

—DAVID RUBINSTEIN
University of Illinois

❑ "The pathology of the black lower class has grown and festered for 40 years, and it will not be solved in four. But we will never solve it if we do not begin. However limited our knowledge, surely it is not beyond our capacity to extend the rule of law, the protection of bodily safety to all citizens of the United States. Surely we can impose some minimal discipline within which a reconstruction of decent life can begin. Surely we can give such a token of our commitment to our fellow citizens, that their American children may live. Yet we do not."[41]

—ADAM WALINSKY
National Committee for the
Police Corps

Juvenile Violent Crime

❏ *Since 1965, the juvenile arrest rate for violent crimes has tripled.*

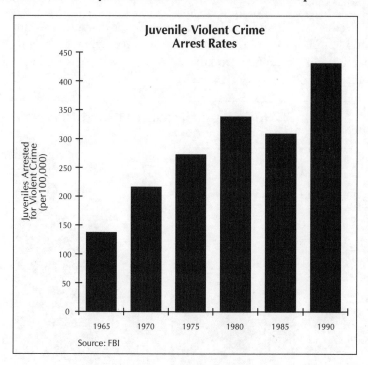

Juvenile Violent Crime Arrest Rates

Source: FBI

Year	Arrest Rates (per 100,000)
1960	NA
1965	137.0
1970	215.9
1975	272.4
1980	338.1
1985	308.6
1990	430.6

Source: FBI

Factual Overview: Juvenile Violent Crime

❑ The fastest growing segment of the criminal population is our nation's children.[42]

❑ Between 1982 and 1991, the arrest rate for juveniles for murder increased 93 percent, the arrest rate for aggravated assault increased 72 percent, for forcible rape 24 percent, and for motor vehicle theft 97 percent.[43]

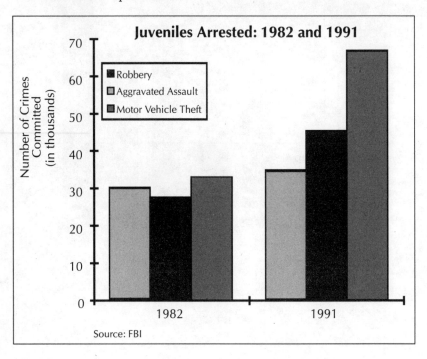

Source: FBI

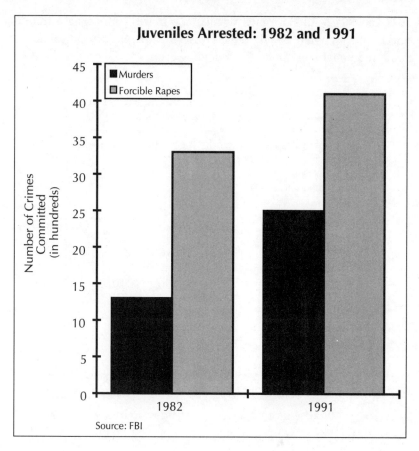

Juveniles Arrested: 1982 and 1991

Number of Crimes Committed (in hundreds)

■ Murders
☐ Forcible Rapes

Source: FBI

❏ Because the population group of 10- to 17-year-olds is going to increase significantly in the 1990s, the violent upsurge will probably accelerate.[44]

❏ There has been a 1,740 percent rise in the number of children and teenagers treated for knife and gunshot wounds since 1986 at the Children's National Medical Center in Washington.[45]

❏ About 3 million thefts and violent crimes occur on or near a school campus each year, representing nearly 16,000 incidents per day.[46]

❏ Twenty percent of high school students now carry a firearm, knife, razor, club, or some other weapon on a regular basis.[47]

❏ In 1991, children under age 10 committed more than 1,000 acts of aggravated assault and 81 cases of forcible rape. Juveniles 12 and under committed the following crimes:[48]

Offenses Committed by Juveniles Under 12: 1991		
Type of Offense	Under Age 10	Ages 10–12
Murder	6	29
Forcible Rape	81	441
Robbery	238	1,924
Motor Vehicle Theft	253	2,423
Aggravated Assault	1,068	3,859
Arson	1,068	1,571
Burglary	3,395	11,959
Larceny-Theft	11,663	50,505
Source: FBI		

❏ In 1991, the violent crime arrest rate for African-American youth was five times higher than that of white youth.[49]

❏ Today, 70 percent of the juvenile offenders in long-term correctional facilities grew up without a father in the household.[50]

❏ Only 5 percent of all young violent offenders are tried as adults. In many states a youthful offender under the age of 16 cannot be sentenced past the age of 25 no matter how serious the crime.[51]

Commentary on Juvenile Violent Crime

❏ "When asked to name a cause for the increase in youth violence, law enforcement officials largely single out the nation's system of so-called juvenile justice. Set up some 30 years ago to protect immature kids who might get arrested for truancy, shoplifting or joy riding, it is ill equipped to deal with the violent children of the 1990s who are robbing, raping and murdering."[52]

—The Wall Street Journal

❏ "Crime does not wash over all Americans equally. It especially terrorizes the weakest and most vulnerable among us. Three quarters of America's 64 million children live in metropolitan areas, a fifth live in low-income households, at least a tenth come home after school to a house containing no adult, and all are physically immature and incompletely formed in character. These are the people who suffer most when law and order decay. Children need order. Aside from love and sustenance, there is nothing they need more than order."[53]

—KARL ZINSMEISTER
American Enterprise Institute

Punishment

❏ **The expected prison sentence for all serious crimes has decreased more than 60 percent since 1954.**

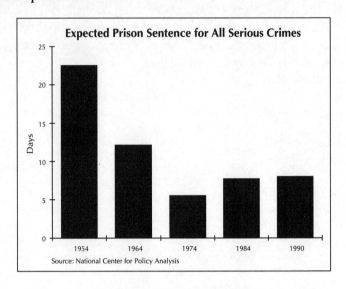

Expected Prison Sentence for All Serious Crimes

Days

Source: National Center for Policy Analysis

Expected Prison Sentence for All Serious Crimes*

Year	Expected Time in Prison (in days)
1954	22.5
1964	12.1
1974	5.5
1984	7.7
1990	8.0

Source: National Center for Policy Analysis

*The "expected punishment" is calculated by multiplying four probabilities (of being arrested, of being prosecuted, of being convicted if prosecuted, and of going to prison if convicted) and then multiplying the product by the median time served for an offense.

Factual Overview: Incarceration and Sentencing

❏ Nearly three out of every four convicted criminals are not incarcerated. In 1990, 62 percent of the estimated 4.3 million persons in correctional custody in the United States were on probation, and 12 percent were on parole.[54]

❏ Fewer than 1 in 10 serious crimes results in imprisonment.[55]

❏ In 1992, the median prison sentence for murder was about 15 years, while the average time served was a little more than 5 years:[56]

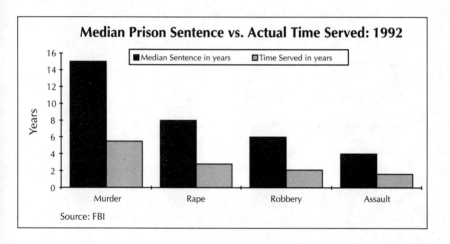

❏ The U.S. imprisons a larger share of its population than any other nation. The American incarceration rate is 455 people per 100,000. This rate is 10 times higher than that of Japan, Sweden, Ireland, and the Netherlands.[57]

❏ In 1992, for every 100,000 inhabitants of the United States, 5,666 persons were arrested.[58]

❏ In 1990, the expected punishment for someone committing a murder was 1.8 years in prison; for rape, the expected sentence was 60 days; for robbery, 23 days; and for aggravated assault, 6.4 days.[59]

❑ Fewer than one in three crimes is reported to the police. Of that one in three, police make an arrest only 20 percent of the time. Nearly half of the people arrested have their charges thrown out by the prosecutor. When you take into account probation and other factors, one person goes to federal prison and one person goes to nonfederal jail for every 100 crimes committed.[60]

Factual Overview: Recidivism

❑ Most prisoners are violent or repeat offenders—93 percent are violent, repeat, or violent repeat offenders.[61]

❑ Of all inmates released from state prison in 1983, 63 percent committed a felony or serious misdemeanor within three years of their release.[62]

Factual Overview: Cost of Crime

❑ According to the Bureau of Justice Statistics, the direct economic cost to crime victims totaled $19.2 billion in 1990.[63]

❑ A conservative, lower-bound estimate of the social cost per crime is about $2,500. Thus, the typical prisoner when free can be said to cost society well over $25,000 per year—he commits approximately 15 crimes a year, each of them representing about $2,500 in social cost. For most prisoners, therefore, the social benefits of incarceration are at least one and one-half times the social costs of incarceration ($25,000 versus 15 times $2,500 or $37,500). If drug crimes are factored in the calculation (which is not now the case) the estimated social benefits of incarceration soar much higher.[64]

Commentary on Punishment

❑ "It may be true that the law cannot make a man love me. But it can keep him from lynching me, and I think that's pretty important."[65]

—REV. MARTIN LUTHER KING, JR.

❏ "There is so much crime without punishment in America today because recent generations of social and political elites, both liberal and conservative, have liberated themselves from the belief that criminals are free moral agents and that publicly sanctioned punishments are what they justly deserve."[66]

—JOHN J. DIIULIO, JR.
Princeton University

❏ "It is clearly more appealing to think of solving the criminal problem by means that are themselves not particularly unpleasant than to think of solving it by methods that *are* unpleasant. But in this case we do not have the choice between a pleasant and an unpleasant method of dealing with crime. We have an unpleasant method—deterrence—that works, and a pleasant method—rehabilitation—that (at least so far) never has worked. Under the circumstances, we have to opt either for the deterrence method or for a higher crime rate."[67]

—GORDON TULLOCK
University of Arizona

❏ "We should understand punishment as a kind of mirror image of praise. If praise expresses gratitude and approbation, punishment expresses resentment and reprobation. If praise expresses what the political community admires and what unites it, punishment expresses what the community condemns and what threatens it. Punishment, like praise, publicly expresses our determination of what people deserve."[68]

—STANLEY BRUBAKER
Colgate University

Drug Use

❏ **Overall drug use among Americans is down more than 50 percent from its peak in the late 1970s.**

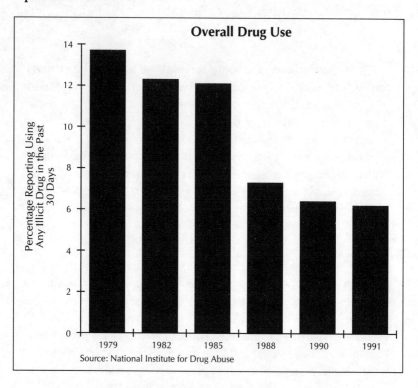

Overall Drug Use

Source: National Institute for Drug Abuse

Percentage of All Americans Reporting Using Drugs in the Past 30 Days

Year	Any Illicit Drug	Marijuana	Cocaine
1979	13.7	12.7	2.4
1982	12.3	11.0	2.3
1985	12.1	9.4	2.9
1988	7.3	5.9	1.5
1990	6.4	5.1	0.8
1991	6.2	4.8	0.9

Source: National Institute for Drug Abuse

Factual Overview: Overall Drug Use Trends

❑ The number of current drug users (that is, persons reporting use of any illicit drug during the past month), is now half of what is was at its peak in 1979.[69]

❑ Nevertheless, nationwide, the number of hard-core addicts remains relatively constant. Between 1988 and 1991, the number of cocaine addicts has remained relatively constant at 860,000. All told, there are approximately 1.5 to 2.5 million cocaine and crack cocaine users.[70]

❑ After a decline in the number of drug-related emergency room visits for cocaine and heroin from 1989 to 1991, 1992 rates have increased.[71]

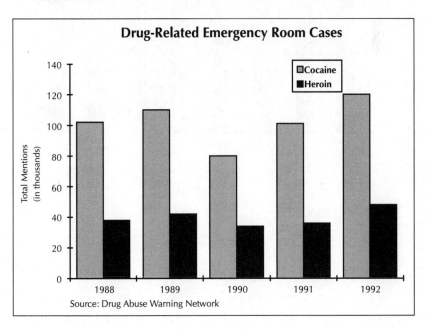

❑ Approximately 25 percent of drug users consume 75 percent of all illegal drugs consumed in the United States, and these hard-core users are the most resistant to anti–drug use strategies.[72]

❏ *Among adolescents, drug and alcohol use is at its lowest point since monitoring began in 1975.*

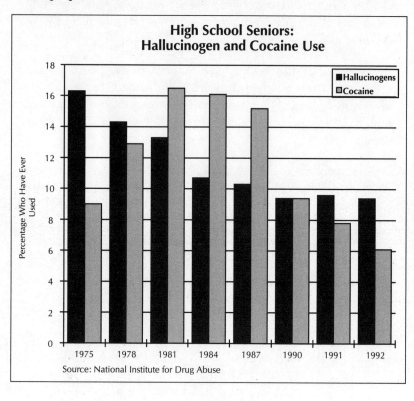

High School Seniors:
Hallucinogen and Cocaine Use

Source: National Institute for Drug Abuse

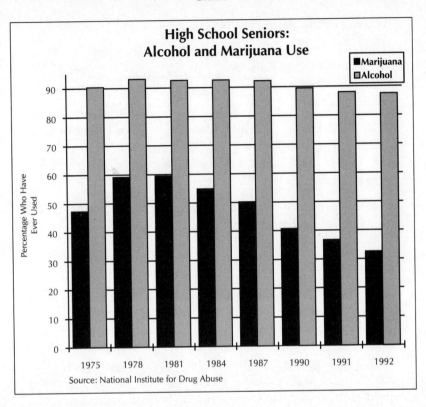

High School Seniors:
Alcohol and Marijuana Use

Source: National Institute for Drug Abuse

NIDA High School Survey on Drug and Alcohol Use (percentage of high school seniors who have ever used)				
Class	Alcohol	Marijuana	Cocaine	Hallucinogens
1975	90.4	47.3	9.0	16.3
1978	93.1	59.2	12.9	14.3
1981	92.6	59.5	16.5	13.3
1984	92.6	54.9	16.1	10.7
1987	92.2	50.2	15.2	10.3
1990	89.5	40.7	9.4	9.4
1991	88.0	36.7	7.8	9.6
1992	87.5	32.6	6.1	9.4

Source: National Institute for Drug Abuse

Factual Overview: Adolescent Drug Use Trends

❏ In 1992, among eighth-grade students nationwide, 11.2 percent reported trying marijuana, 1 percentage point higher than in 1991. In addition, LSD use among eighth-graders increased 24 percent from 1991.[73]

❏ In 1991, 134,000 teenagers used cocaine once a week or more and 580,000 teenagers used marijuana once a week or more. In addition, 454,000 junior and senior high school students were weekly binge drinkers.[74]

❏ In 1990, an estimated 1.6 million American teenagers needed treatment for alcohol and other drug abuse.[75]

Commentary on Drug Use

❏ "Even now, when the dangers of drug abuse are well understood, many educated people still discuss the drug problem in almost every way except the right way. They talk about the 'costs' of drug use and the 'socioeconomic factors' that shape that use. They rarely speak plainly—drug use is wrong because it is immoral and it is immoral because it enslaves the mind and destroys the soul. It is as if it were a mark of sophistication for us to shun the language of morality in discussing the problems of mankind."[76]

—JAMES Q. WILSON
University of California,
Los Angeles

❏ "Many of the young people involved in the drug trade do so because the risk of prosecution does not act as a deterrent. Knowing that a conviction in juvenile court will in all probability result in little or no punishment, the benefits...outweigh the risks.... We must not permit this situation to continue."[77]

—JUDGE REGGIE WALTON
Superior Court of the
District of Columbia

Chapter 2

Family and Children

Factual Overview: The Family

❏ In 1960, the average family in America had four family members and a median family income (in constant 1991 dollars) of $25,000.[1] The average family in the early 1990s has three members and a median family income of $35,000.[2]

❏ Between 1960 and 1991 the size of the child population in the United States was relatively constant at 64 million children.[3]

❏ In 1960, children constituted 36 percent of the U. S. population; in 1991, they constituted 27 percent.[4]

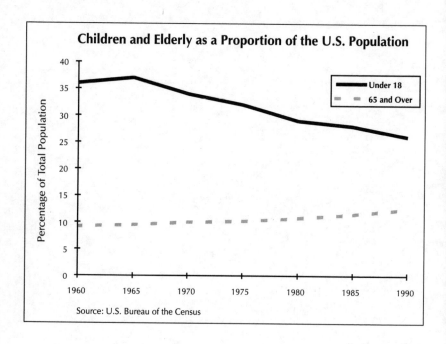

Children and Elderly as a Proportion of the U.S. Population

Source: U.S. Bureau of the Census

❏ Between the mid-1950s and the mid-1970s, the average number of births per woman dropped from 3.7 to 1.8, and it has increased only slightly in recent years.[5]

❏ Between 1960 and 1991 total spending per child (adjusted for inflation) on services such as schools and health care more than doubled.[6]

Commentary on the Family

❏ "The family is the cornerstone of our society. More than any other force it shapes the attitude, the hopes, the ambitions, and the values of the child. And when the family collapses, it is the children that are usually damaged. When it happens on a massive scale the community itself is crippled."[7]

—PRESIDENT LYNDON JOHNSON
at Howard University, 1965

❏ "There is a mountain of scientific evidence showing that when families disintegrate, children often end up with intellectual, physical and emotional scars that persist for life. . . . We talk about the drug crisis, the education crisis, and the problem of teen pregnancy and juvenile crime. But all these ills trace back predominantly to one source: broken families."[8]

—KARL ZINSMEISTER
American Enterprise Institute

❏ "Americans suspect that the nation's economic difficulties are rooted not in technical economic forces (for example, exchange rates or capital formation) but in fundamental moral causes. There exists a deeply intuitive sense that the success of a market-based economy depends on a highly developed social morality—trustworthiness, honesty, concern for future generations, an ethic of service to others, a humane society that takes care of those in need, frugality instead of greed, high standards of quality and concern for community. These economically desirable social values, in turn, are seen as rooted in family values. Thus the link in public thinking between a healthy family and a robust economy, though indirect, is clear and firm."[9]

—DANIEL YANKELOVICH
Public Agenda Foundation

Illegitimate Births

❑ **Since 1960, illegitimate birth rates have increased more than 400 percent.**

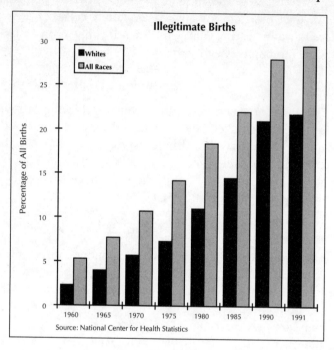

Illegitimate Births

Year	Percentage of All Births (all races)	Percentage of All Births (whites)	Percentage of All Births (blacks)
1960	5.3	2.3	23.0
1965	7.7	4.0	27.9
1970	10.7	5.7	37.6
1975	14.2	7.3	48.8
1980	18.4	11.0	55.2
1985	22.0	14.5	60.1
1990	28.0	21.0	65.2
1991	29.5	21.8	67.9

Source: National Center for Health Statistics

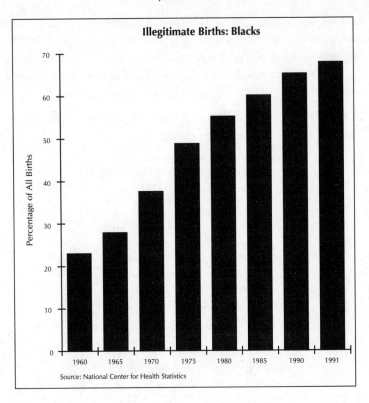

Illegitimate Births: Blacks

Source: National Center for Health Statistics

Factual Overview: Illegitimate Births

❑ In 1960, 5 percent of all births were out of wedlock. By 1991, 30 percent of all births were illegitimate. Among whites, the numbers increased from 2 percent of all births in 1960 to 22 percent of all births in 1991. Among blacks, the numbers increased from 23 percent in 1960 to 68 percent in 1991.[10]

❑ By 2000, according to some projections, 40 percent of all American births and 80 percent of minority births will occur out of wedlock.[11]

❑ In 1961 and 1991, roughly the same number of babies were born (about 4 million)—but in 1991, five times as many of them were born out of wedlock.[12]

❑ The rate of illegitimacy has increased nearly 60 percent in the last decade alone. Almost one-quarter of all unmarried women in the United States become unwed mothers. And the largest proportional increase is among well-educated, affluent women, suggesting that the social stigma on illegitimacy is disappearing.[13]

❑ In 1991, in 10 major cities in the United States, more than 50 percent of all births were illegitimate.[14]

Rate of Illegitimacy in Ten Major U.S. Cities: 1991	
City	Percentage of Illegitimate Births (all races)
Detroit	71.0
Washington, D.C.	66.3
St. Louis	65.9
Newark	64.7
Atlanta	64.4
Cleveland	64.1
Baltimore	62.1
Philadelphia	59.4
Chicago	54.7
Pittsburgh	51.9

Source: National Center for Health Statistics

Commentary on Illegitimate Births

❑ "Illegitimacy is the single most important social problem of our time—more important than crime, drugs, poverty, illiteracy, welfare or homelessness because it drives everything else."[15]

—CHARLES MURRAY
author, Losing Ground

❏ "[T]he public costs of having children out of wedlock are very high. Children born out of wedlock tend to have high infant mortality, low birth weight (with attendant morbidities), and high probabilities of being poor, not completing school, and staying on welfare themselves. As a matter of public policy, if not of morality, it pays for society to approve of marriage as the best setting for children, and to discourage having children out of wedlock."[16]

—MICHAEL NOVAK
author, The Catholic Ethic and the
Spirit of Capitalism

❏ "The fact that Washington and Harlem have 80 percent illegitimacy has nothing to do with racism in America. It has to do with 13-, 14-, and 15-year old girls having sexual intercourse without the benefit of marriage. In 1925, 85 percent of black kids lived in two-parent families. Surely in Harlem in 1925, blacks were far poorer and there was more discrimination."[17]

—WALTER WILLIAMS
George Mason University

❏ "If we fail to come to terms with the relationship between family structure and declining child well-being, then it will be increasingly difficult to improve children's life prospects, no matter how many new programs the federal government funds. Nor will we be able to make progress in bettering school performance or reducing crime or improving the quality of the nation's future work force—all domestic problems closely connected to family breakup. Worse, we may contribute to the problem by pursuing policies that actually increase family instability and breakup."[18]

—BARBARA DAFOE WHITEHEAD
Institute for American Values

Single-Parent Families

❏ **Since 1960, the percentage of families headed by a single parent has more than tripled.**

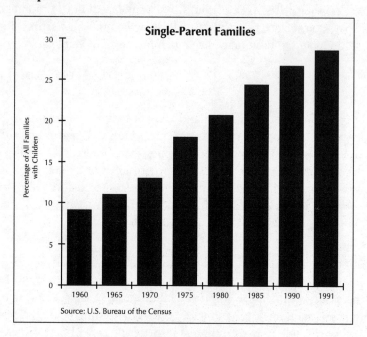

Source: U.S. Bureau of the Census

Single-Parent Families	
Year	Single-Parent Families (as a percentage of all families with children)
1960	9.1
1965	11.0
1970	13.0
1975	18.0
1980	20.7
1985	24.4
1990	26.7
1991	28.6

Source: U.S. Bureau of the Census

Factual Overview: Single-Parent Families

❑ By 1992, non-marital childbearing had reached near parity with divorce as a social generator of female-headed homes. If current trends continue, sometime during the mid-1990s the total number of fatherless homes created by unwed childbearing will surpass the number created by divorce.[19]

❑ Approximately 90 percent of single-parent homes are homes without a father.[20]

❑ Since 1960, the percentage of children living with both biological parents from birth through age 18 has dropped 22 percentage points.[21]

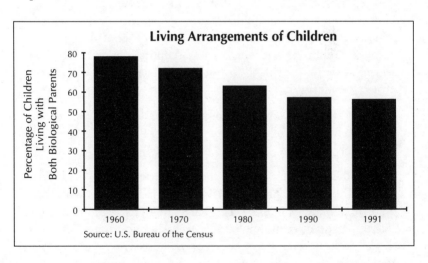

Living Arrangements of Children

Percentage of Children Living with Both Biological Parents

Source: U.S. Bureau of the Census

❑ According to some projections, only 6 percent of black children and 30 percent of white children born in 1980 will live with both parents through age 18. By comparison, for children born in 1950, 52 percent of black children and 81 percent of white children lived with both parents through age 18.[22]

Factual Overview: Impact of Single-Parent Families

❑ Children from single-parent families are two to three times as likely as children in two-parent families to have emotional and behavioral problems. In addition, they are more likely to drop out of high school, become pregnant as teenagers, abuse drugs, and become entangled with the law.[23]

❑ Eighteen- to twenty-two-year-olds from disrupted families are more likely to have poor relationships with their fathers and mothers, to show high levels of emotional and behavior problems, to have received psychological help, and to have dropped out of high school. Disruption-related problems are more apparent in young adulthood than they were in adolescence, especially among females. Young women from disrupted families are more likely to have disturbed mother-child relationships and to receive psychological help, while males show more school dropout and problem behavior. Youth experiencing early disruption (prior to age six) are particularly at risk. And overall, remarriage does not have a protective effect.[24]

❑ According to a study of whites, daughters of single parents are 164 percent more likely to have a premarital birth, and 92 percent more likely to dissolve their own marriages.[25]

❑ Half the single mothers in the United States live below the poverty line, while only about 1 in 10 married couples with children are poor. Regardless of class, single mothers are more vulnerable to persistent economic insecurity. A significant number of all single mothers never marry or remarry. Those who do, do so only after spending roughly six years, on average, as single parents.[26]

❑ Single-parent families earn dramatically less each year than two-parent families:[27]

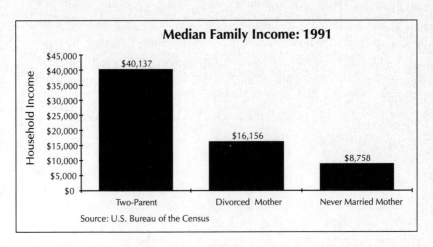

Median Family Income: 1991

Two-Parent: $40,137
Divorced Mother: $16,156
Never Married Mother: $8,758

Source: U.S. Bureau of the Census

Commentary on Single-Parent Families

❑ "From the wild Irish slums of the 19th century Eastern seaboard to the riot-torn suburbs of Los Angeles, there is one unmistakable lesson in American history: A community that allows a large number of young men to grow up in broken families, dominated by women, never acquiring any stable relationship to male authority, never acquiring any rational expectations about the future—that community asks for and gets chaos. . . . [In such a society] crime, violence, unrest, unrestrained lashing out at the whole social structure—these are not only to be expected, they are very nearly inevitable."[28]

—DANIEL PATRICK MOYNIHAN
Assistant Secretary of Labor, 1965

❑ "I know of few other bodies of data in which the weight of evidence is so decisively on one side of the issue: on the whole, for children, two-parent families are preferable. . . . If our prevailing views on family structure hinged solely on scholarly evidence, the current debate never would have arisen in the first place."[29]

—DAVID POPENOE
Rutgers University

❏ "Now that the mass media, the schools, and even the churches have begun to treat single parenthood as a regrettable but inescapable part of modern life, we can hardly expect respectable poor to carry on the struggle against illegitimacy and desertion with their old fervor. They still deplore such behavior, but they cannot make it morally taboo. Once the two-parent norm loses its moral sanctity, the selfish considerations that always pulled poor parents apart often become overwhelming."[30]

—CHRISTOPHER JENCKS
Northwestern University

❏ "The economic consequences of a parent's absence are often accompanied by psychological consequences, which include higher than average levels of youth suicide, low intellectual and educational performance, and higher than average rates of mental illness, violence and drug use."[31]

—WILLIAM GALSTON
and ELAINE KAMARCK
Deputy Assistant to President
Clinton for Domestic Policy
Senior Policy Advisor
to Vice President Gore

Marriage

❑ **The rate at which people are getting married is more than 25 percent lower than in 1960.**

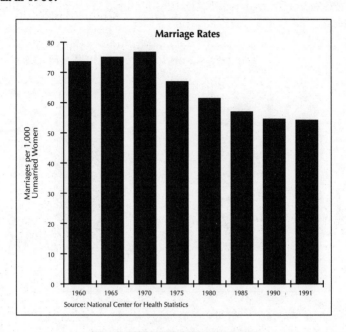

Marriage Rates

Marriages per 1,000 Unmarried Women

Source: National Center for Health Statistics

Marriage Rates	
Year	Rate of Unmarried Women (per 1,000)
1960	73.5
1965	75.0
1970	76.7
1975	66.9
1980	61.4
1985	57.0
1990	54.6
1991	54.2

Source: National Center for Health Statistics

Factual Overview: Marriage

❏ In 1960 there were 74 marriages for every 1,000 unmarried women and 9 divorces for every 1,000 married women. By 1991, there were 54 marriages per 1,000 unmarried women and 21 divorces per 1,000 married women.[32]

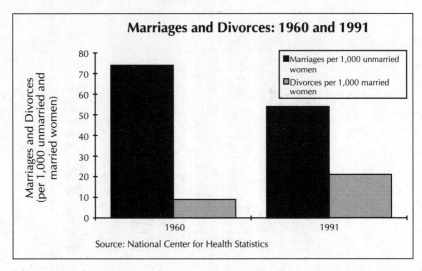

Marriages and Divorces: 1960 and 1991

Source: National Center for Health Statistics

❏ Married couples make up the smallest percentage of the nation's households in two centuries. Married couples make up 55 percent of the nation's 91.9 million households, down from 60 percent in the 1980 census.[33]

❏ Two-parent households provide increased supervision and guardianship not only for their own children and household property, but also for general activities in the community. From this perspective, the supervision of peer-group and gang activity is not simply dependent on one child's family, but on a network of collective family control.[34]

Commentary on Marriage

❑ "The contemporary legal system views people as autonomous individuals endowed with rights and entering into real or implied contracts. The liberalization of laws pertaining to marriage and divorce arose out of just such a view. Marriage, once a sacrament, has become in the eyes of the law a contract that is easily negotiated, renegotiated, or rescinded. Within a few years, no-fault divorce on demand became possible, after millennia in which such an idea would have been unthinkable. It is now easier to renounce a marriage than a mortgage; at least the former occurs much more frequently than the latter. Half of all divorced fathers rarely see their children, and most pay no child support."[35]

—JAMES Q. WILSON
University of California,
Los Angeles

Divorce

❏ **The divorce rate has decreased from its peak in the early 1980s; however, the divorce rate has more than doubled since 1960.**

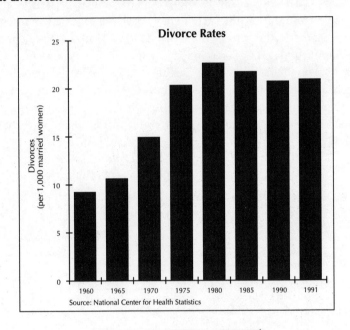

Divorce Rates

Source: National Center for Health Statistics

Divorces	
Year	Rate per Married Women (per 1,000)
1960	9.2
1965	10.6
1970	14.9
1975	20.3
1980	22.6
1985	21.7
1990	20.7
1991	20.9

Source: National Center for Health Statistics

Factual Overview: Divorce

❏ More than half of divorces involve children. Over 1 million children yearly have parents who separate or divorce.[36]

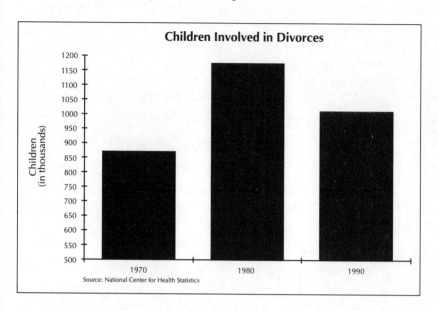

Children Involved in Divorces

Children (in thousands)

1200
1150
1100
1050
1000
950
900
850
800
750
700
650
600
550
500

1970   1980   1990

Source: National Center for Health Statistics

❏ The United States has the highest divorce rate in the world. At present rates, approximately half of all U.S. marriages can be expected to end in divorce.[37]

❏ Both cohabiting and remarried couples are more likely to break up than couples in first marriages.[38]

❏ Divorce has its most significant repercussions on girls with regard to future marital stability: a 1987 study found that white women who were younger than 16 when their parents divorced or separated were about 60 percent more likely to be divorced and separated themselves.[39]

Commentary on Divorce

❏ "The sequence of divorce followed by a succession of boy or girlfriends, a second marriage, and frequently another divorce and another turnover of partners often means a repeatedly disrupted educational coalition. Each change in participants involves a change in the educational agenda for the child. Each new partner cannot be expected to pick up the previous one's education post and program. . . . As a result, changes in parenting partners mean, at best, a deep disruption in a child's education, though of course several disruptions cut deeper into the effectiveness of the educational coalition than just one."[40]

—AMITAI ETZIONI
George Washington University

❏ "Because of the shattering emotional and developmental effects of divorce on children, it would be reasonable to introduce 'braking' mechanisms that require parents contemplating divorce to pause for reflection."[41]

—WILLIAM GALSTON and
ELAINE KAMARCK
Deputy Assistant to President
Clinton for Domestic Policy
Senior Policy Advisor
to Vice President Gore

Child Poverty

❏ Since 1960, the number of children in poverty has dropped 17 percent, though since 1970, the number of children in poverty has increased 40 percent.

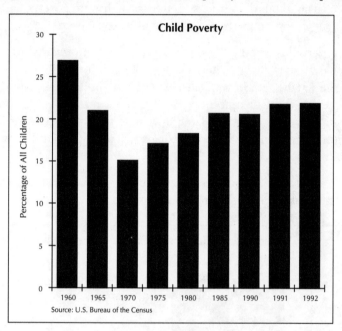

Child Poverty

Percentage of All Children

Source: U.S. Bureau of the Census

Children in Poverty		
Year	Number (millions)	Percentage
1960	17.6	26.9
1965	14.7	21.0
1970	10.4	15.1
1975	11.1	17.1
1980	10.5	18.3
1985	13.0	20.7
1990	13.4	20.6
1991	14.3	21.8
1992	14.6	21.9

Source: U.S. Bureau of the Census

Factual Overview: Child Poverty

❏ In 1970, 10.4 million children lived in poverty; by 1992 that number had increased to 14.6 million.[42]

❏ One child out of every five in the nation lives in poverty, and of all age groups, children are the most likely to be poor.[43]

❏ Poverty historically has derived primarily from unemployment and low wages. Today it derives increasingly from family structure. In the 1980s, the United States experienced an important turning point: for the first time in recent history, a majority of all poor families were one-parent families. Single-parent families are six times more likely to be poor than married-couple families with children.[44]

❏ A child's likelihood of staying in poverty for more than seven years is linked to his or her family structure:[45]

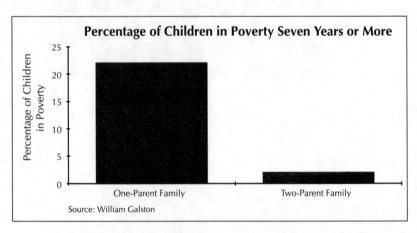

Percentage of Children in Poverty Seven Years or More

Source: William Galston

❏ Twenty-five percent of all fathers required to pay child support do not. Thirty percent of all the child support payments required in the United States are uncollected.[46]

Commentary on Child Poverty

❑ "The best anti-poverty program for children is a stable, intact family."[47]

> —WILLIAM GALSTON and
> ELAINE KAMARCK
> Deputy Assistant to President
> Clinton for Domestic Policy
> Senior Policy Advisor
> to Vice President Gore

❑ "The condition of children's lives and their future prospects largely reflect the well-being of their families. When families are strong, stable and loving, children have a sound basis for becoming caring and competent adults. When families are unable to give children the affection and attention they need and to provide for their material needs, children are far less likely to achieve their full potential."[48]

> —National Commission on
> Children, 1991

Welfare

❏ **More than one child in eight is being raised on government welfare through Aid to Families with Dependent Children (AFDC).**

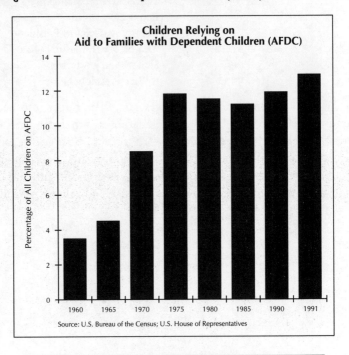

**Children Relying on
Aid to Families with Dependent Children (AFDC)**

Source: U.S. Bureau of the Census; U.S. House of Representatives

Year	Children Relying on AFDC	
	Percentage of Children on AFDC	Children on AFDC (millions)
1960	3.5	2.37
1965	4.5	3.16
1970	8.5	6.10
1975	11.8	7.95
1980	11.5	7.26
1985	11.2	7.07
1990	11.9	7.62
1991	12.9	8.38

Source: U.S. Bureau of the Census; U.S. House of Representatives

Factual Overview: Welfare

❏ During the 1970s, the number of recipients of AFDC rose from nearly 2 million to more than 3.5 million. The number dropped at the start of the 1980s, before beginning to grow again. By 1990, the number of AFDC recipients nationwide was 4.6 million. The number of Food Stamp recipients has climbed as well, quintupling between 1970 and 1980—from 4.3 million to 21.1 million.[49]

❏ In order for a single mother to get her welfare "paycheck" she must meet two conditions: 1) she must not work; 2) she must not marry an employed male.[50]

❏ About 50 percent of all unwed teenage mothers go on welfare within one year of the birth of their first child. More than 75 percent go on within five years.[51]

❏ Almost-one quarter (22.1 percent) of children born in the late 1960s were dependent on AFDC for at least one year of their life before reaching their 18th birthday.[52]

❏ By race, 72.3 percent of black children and 15.7 percent of non-black children were supported by AFDC at one point or another during childhood.[53]

❏ Fifty-three percent of AFDC recipients are off welfare before two years, 26 percent stay on for two to five years, and 22 percent continue to receive AFDC payments for more than five years.[54]

❏ In the 1950s, before the "War on Poverty" was launched as part of Lyndon Johnson's Great Society, nearly one-third of all poor families were headed by adults who worked full-time during the year. In 1990, only 15 percent of all poor families had working heads of households. Half of poor, non-elderly adults do not work at all.[55]

Factual Overview: Social and Welfare Spending

❑ Total social spending* by the federal government, in constant 1990 dollars, has increased from $144 billion in 1960 to $787 billion in 1990:[56]

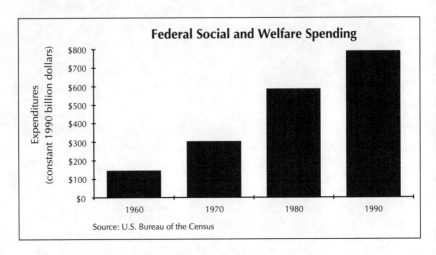

Federal Social and Welfare Spending

Expenditures (constant 1990 billion dollars)

Source: U.S. Bureau of the Census

❑ The percentage of social spending as part of America's Gross National Product (GNP) has increased from 6.7 percent in 1960 to 14.4 percent in 1990.[57]

❑ Federal expenditures on means-tested welfare programs have risen over 700 percent in the past 30 years, from $29 billion in 1960 to $212 billion in 1990 (in constant 1990 dollars).[58]

Commentary on Welfare

❑ "After making the most arduous attempt to objectify the problem of poverty, to divorce poverty from any moral assumptions and conditions, we are learning how inseparable the moral and material dimensions of that problem are. And after trying to devise

---

*Total social spending includes transfer payments assisting the general population such as Social Security and Medicare, as well as conventional welfare programs targeted at low-income persons such as Food Stamps and Aid to Families with Dependent Children.

social policies that are scrupulously neutral and 'value free,' we are finding these policies fraught with moral implications that have grave material and social consequences."[59]

—GERTRUDE HIMMELFARB
author, *Poverty and Compassion*

❏ "What makes the underclass different not just from you but also from the majority of the poor both today and in the past is its self-defeating behavior and the worldview from which that behavior springs.... The underclass is equipped with different, and sparser, mental and emotional furniture, unhelpful for taking advantage of the economic opportunities that American life offers."[60]

—MYRON MAGNET
author, *The Dream and the Nightmare*

❏ "[B]eginning in the early 60's... American social policy toward poor and disadvantaged youths underwent a transformation.... Poverty, it was concluded, is caused by structural features of capitalism. If a student misbehaves in school or a young man snatches a purse or a young woman has a baby without a husband, these are expressions of or responses to social conditions beyond their control. Value judgments themselves are inappropriate. Having a baby without a husband is a choice, not a sin or even necessarily a mistake. It is society that must change, not individuals; the rich must see the errors of their ways, not the poor the errors of theirs. To hold people accountable for their behavior is unjust—blaming the victim. Root causes must be corrected. These views permeated every reform that affected poor people, and especially poor black young people, and there were hundreds of such reforms. They consisted not only of new laws and offices and bureaus and programs, but also of dozens of landmark court decisions, sweeping executive actions, and obscure changes in regulatory and administrative practice that sometimes had wide repercussions."[61]

—CHARLES MURRAY
author, *Losing Ground*

Abortion

❑ **Since 1972, there have been more than 28 million abortions in the United States. Today, nearly one in four pregnancies ends in abortion.**

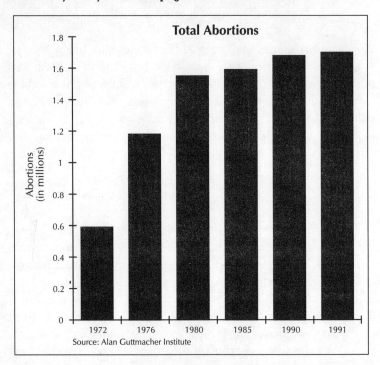

Total Abortions

Source: Alan Guttmacher Institute

Abortions	
Year	Number (in millions)
1972	.6
1976	1.2
1980	1.6
1985	1.6
1990	1.7
1991	1.7

Source: Alan Guttmacher Institute

Factual Overview: Abortion

❏ More than 40 percent of abortions are performed on women who have had one or more abortions before.[62]

❏ According to the Alan Guttmacher Institute:[63]

Abortions by Age Group	
Age Group	Percentage of Total Abortions
Under 20	26
20–24	33
25–29	21
30–34	12
35–39	6
40 and up	1

Abortions by Marital Status	
Marital Status	Percentage of Total Abortions
Never Married	63
Married	19
Divorced	11
Separated	6
Widowed	1

❏ Eighty-three percent of abortions are performed on white females, and 17 percent on minority women.[64]

❏ Among girls under the age of 15, the abortion rate increased by 18 percent between 1980 and 1987. The number of abortions in this age group also increased while the population decreased by nearly 215,000.[65]

❏ Unmarried women are more than five times as likely to have an abortion than married women.[66]

❏ There are nearly 200,000 second- and third-trimester abortions every year.[67]

❏ Only 7 percent of all abortions fall into the category of threatened life of the mother, health of the child, and victim of rape or incest.[68]

Commentary on Abortion

❏ "Very few Americans believe that all abortions all the time are all right. Almost all Americans believe that abortions should be illegal when the children can live without the mother's assistance, when the children can live outside the mother's womb."[69]

—PRESIDENT BILL CLINTON

❏ "Neither the [German] Bundestag nor any other Western legislature has gone so far as *Roe v. Wade*, which tolerates no significant fetal protection measures before viability (roughly the first six months) and forbids any restriction thereafter that burdens the health, broadly defined, of the woman seeking abortion. The experience of other liberal democracies... throws into high relief the extremism of America's judge-made abortion law: In Western nations where abortion policy has been left up to the people and their elected representatives, all the compromises that have emerged have been more protective of unborn life than *Roe v. Wade*."[70]

—MARY ANN GLENDON
Harvard Law School

❏ "[C]ontrary to established opinion, the disagreement over abortion is not, at root, a legal one. Law is neither the fundamental problem nor the final solution. Thus if abortion rights advocates think that their opposition will just get tired some day and go away, they are dreaming—as are anti-abortion advocates if they imagine that all will be well the moment *Roe v. Wade* is overturned. None of the various possible legal outcomes will settle the dispute or even ease the tensions between these two groups, because the abortion controversy is in its nature a cultural controversy. No matter what happens in courts and legislatures the abortion issue will not disappear until we somehow reach a greater consensus with respect to the standards of justice and goodness our communities will abide by. If there is to be an abortion law that is politically sustainable over the long haul, then, the fundamental task must be one of moral suasion."[71]

—JAMES DAVISON HUNTER
University of Virginia

Chapter 3

Youth: Pathologies and Behavior

Births to Unmarried Teenagers

❏ **The rate of births to unmarried teenagers has increased almost 200 percent since 1960.**

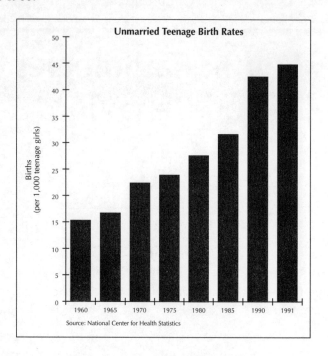

Unmarried Teenage Birth Rates

Births
(per 1,000 teenage girls)

Source: National Center for Health Statistics

Unmarried Teenage Birth Rates	
Year	Rate (per 1,000 teenage girls)
1960	15.3
1965	16.7
1970	22.4
1975	23.9
1980	27.6
1985	31.6
1990	42.5
1991	44.8

Source: National Center for Health Statistics

Factual Overview: Births to Unmarried Teens

❏ In 1990, more than two-thirds of all births to teens are to unmarried girls, compared to less than one-third in 1970.[1]

❏ Over the past several decades, the number of births to married teens has fallen dramatically, from 456,600 in 1970 to 172,800 in 1990. The number of births to unmarried teens has been increasing for more than a decade in all age groups.[2]

❏ Becoming a parent as a teenager increases the chances that a young mother will not complete high school, that she will fare poorly in the job market, and that she and her children will live in poverty.[3]

Commentary on Unmarried Teenage Birth Rates

❏ "Every 64 seconds—about the time it takes for an average person to leave the house, get in a car, and back out of the driveway— a baby is born to a teenage mother in this country. Five minutes later, a baby will have been born to a teenager who already has a child. Ten hours later, by the time this person perhaps returns home from work, more than 560 babies will have been born to teenagers in America. Adolescent pregnancy, which for too many young people begins or perpetuates a cycle of poverty, remains a crisis in America."[4]

—Children's Defense Fund

❏ "When teenagers have babies both mothers and children tend to have problems—health, social, psychological, and economic. Teens who have children out of wedlock are more likely to end up at the bottom of the socio-economic ladder.... These numbers have enormous economic implications for the country—and for the rearing of children in America."[5]

—ALVIN POUSSAINT
Harvard University

Unmarried Teenage Pregnancy and Abortion Rates

❑ **The number of unmarried teenagers getting pregnant has nearly doubled in the past two decades.**

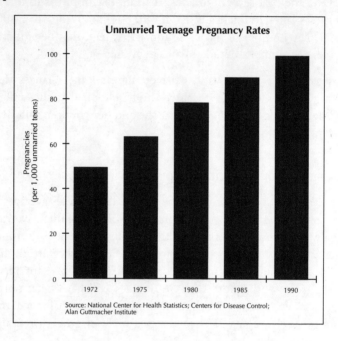

Unmarried Teenage Pregnancy Rates

Source: National Center for Health Statistics; Centers for Disease Control; Alan Guttmacher Institute

Unmarried Teenage Pregnancy Rates

Year	Pregnancies (per 1,000 unmarried teens)
1972	49.4
1975	63.1
1980	78.3
1985	89.6
1988	93.0
1990	99.2

Source: National Center for Health Statistics; Centers for Disease Control; Alan Guttmacher Institute

❑ *Approximately 40 percent of teenage pregnancies, about 400,000 a year, end in abortion. Teens account for more than one-quarter of the total number of abortions in the U.S. annually.*

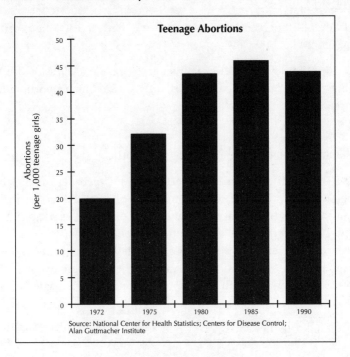

Teenage Abortions

Source: National Center for Health Statistics; Centers for Disease Control; Alan Guttmacher Institute

Teenage Abortions	
Year	Abortions (per 1,000 teenage girls)
1972	19.9
1975	32.1
1980	43.4
1985	45.9
1990	43.8

SOURCE: National Center for Health Statistics; Centers for Disease Control; Alan Guttmacher Institute

Factual Overview: Teenage Pregnancy and Abortion

❑ About 20 percent of teenage girls are expected to have at least one baby by age 20.[6]

❑ About 20 percent of teenage girls will have at least one abortion by age 20.[7]

❑ In 1974, less than half of all teenage pregnancies resulted in an abortion or out-of-wedlock birth. By 1985 the proportion had risen to more than two-thirds.[8]

Commentary on Teenage Pregnancy and Abortion

❑ "Let us listen to parents, teachers, and teenagers themselves before the vastly increased commitment of resources called for by the advocates of contraception and abortion becomes national policy. There needs to be a recognition by public officials at all levels that there are effective approaches to adolescent pregnancy more in keeping with our traditions and values. Without these, we will only continue to pursue with cold illogic the fantasy of a magic bullet."[9]

—EUNICE KENNEDY SHRIVER
Founder and President, Special
Olympics International

❑ "The key to the old system seems to have been that teenagers were held responsible for any children they engendered. They were held accountable by parents and relatives, by neighbors and acquaintances, and by official representatives of the community. . . . More importantly, nonfamilial agencies or third parties have tended to intrude themselves between parents and children, taking over all or part of what traditionally were parental functions and hence assuming parental authority. . . . Teenagers are not only given birth control devices and abortions without parental consent, but are also given 'sex education'—often conveying an implied approval of sexual relations among teenagers as long as a 'method' is used."[10]

—KINGSLEY DAVIS
National Institutes of Health

❏ "The final result to emerge from the analysis is that neither pregnancy education nor contraception education exerts any significant effect on the risk of premarital pregnancy among sexually active teenagers—a finding that calls into question the argument that formal sex education is an effective tool for reducing adolescent pregnancy."[11]

—DEBORAH DAWSON
National Center for Health
Statistics

❏ "[T]here are precautions to be taken by the young and by the unmarried, especially for those who know that they are not remotely close to being ready for the unending responsibility of parenthood. If they want to have a future, it is imperative that our young—male and female alike—embrace the ultimate precaution—abstinence."[12]

—L. DOUGLAS WILDER
Governor of Virginia,
1990–1994

Teenage Suicide

❏ **Since 1960, the rate at which teenagers are taking their own lives has more than tripled. Suicide is now the second leading cause of death among adolescents.**

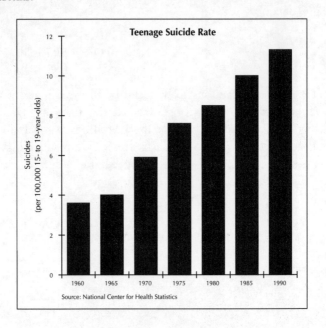

Source: National Center for Health Statistics

Teenage Suicide Rate	
Year	Rate (per 100,000 15- to 19-year-olds)
1960	3.6
1965	4.0
1970	5.9
1975	7.6
1980	8.5
1985	10.0
1990	11.3

Source: National Center for Health Statistics

Factual Overview: Teenage Suicide

❑ The prototypical suicide casualty is no longer an older, depressed male. The rate is rising most rapidly among younger males (five times more numerous than female suicides) who are not usually depressed but are angry, frustrated, resentful, often using drugs and unable to communicate their distress.[13]

❑ For every successful suicide there are at least fifty to one hundred adolescent suicide attempts. Researchers also note that, because of the social stigma associated with suicide, many deaths that are said to be accidents are actually due to suicide.[14]

Chapter 4

Education

Performance, Spending, and School Problems

❏ *While expenditures on elementary and secondary education have increased more than 200 percent since 1960, SAT scores have declined 73 points.*

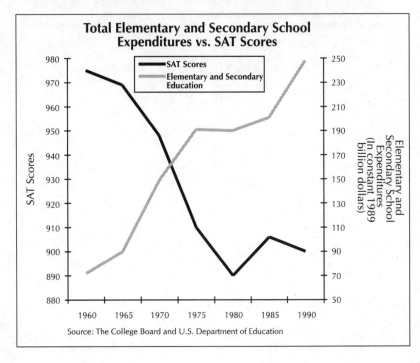

Total Elementary and Secondary School Expenditures vs. SAT Scores

Legend:
- SAT Scores
- Elementary and Secondary Education

Left axis: SAT Scores (880–980)
Right axis: Elementary and Secondary School Expenditures (In constant 1989 billion dollars) (50–250)
X-axis: 1960, 1965, 1970, 1975, 1980, 1985, 1990

Source: The College Board and U.S. Department of Education

❏ There is no systematic correlation between spending on education and student achievement.[1]

Top States in SAT Scores: 1992–93

State	Rank	Expenditure Rank
Iowa	1	27
North Dakota	2	44
South Dakota	3	42
Utah	4	51
Minnesota	5	25

Source: American Legislative Exchange Council and Empower America

Top States in Expenditures: 1992–93

State	Rank	SAT Rank
New Jersey	1	39
Alaska	2	31
Connecticut	3	33
New York	4	40
District of Columbia	5	49

Source: American Legislative Exchange Council and Empower America

❏ Discipline problems in American public schools have gotten much worse over time:[2]

Top Disciplinary Problems According to Public School Teachers

1940	1990
Talking out of turn	Drug Abuse
Chewing gum	Alcohol Abuse
Making noise	Pregnancy
Running in the halls	Suicide
Cutting in line	Rape
Dress-code violations	Robbery
Littering	Assault

Source: Congressional Quarterly

Achievement

❏ *Scholastic Aptitude test scores among all students have dropped 73 points from 1960 to 1993.*

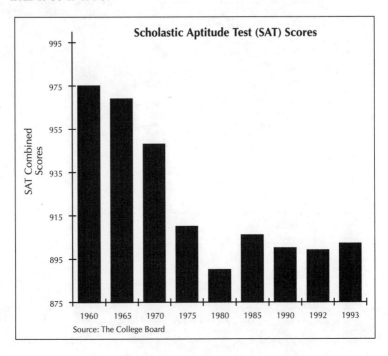

Scholastic Aptitude Test (SAT) Scores

SAT Combined Scores

Source: The College Board

Scholastic Aptitude Test (SAT) Scores			
Year	Verbal	Mathematical	Combined
1960	477	498	975
1965	473	496	969
1970	460	488	948
1975	437	473	910
1980	424	466	890
1985	431	475	906
1990	424	476	900
1992	423	476	899
1993	424	478	902

Source: The College Board

Factual Overview: International Achievement

❏ In a 1989 National Geographic survey of geographical knowledge, Americans between the ages of 18 to 24 finished last among nine countries, including Mexico.[3]

❏ In the 1988 International Assessment of Educational Progress exams in science, U.S. students scored last among tested nations.[4]

1988 International Test Comparison: Science	
Country	Mean Score (0–1,000)
Korea	568
Spain	512
United Kingdom	510
Ireland	504
United States	474
Source: U.S. Department of Education	

❏ But when students were asked about their attitudes toward math and science, more than two-thirds of American students responded that they were "good at math," compared with less than one-quarter of Korean students.[5]

International Assessment of Educational Progress: "I am good at math"	
Country	Percentage responding positively
United States	68
Spain	60
Ireland	49
United Kingdom	47
Korea	23
SOURCE: U.S. Department of Education	

Factual Overview: Educational Achievement

❏ In 1992, 72 percent of fourth-grade students could do third-grade math (addition, subtraction, and simple problem-solving with whole numbers). Twenty percent of eighth-graders could do seventh-grade math (fractions, decimals, percents, and elementary concepts in geometry, statistics, and algebra), and only 6 percent of twelfth-grade students grasped the reasoning and problem solving involving geometric relationships, algebra, and fractions that prepare them for college-level math.[6]

❏ Overall trends in science, mathematics, reading, and writing during the two decades covered by the NAEP (National Assessment of Education Progress) show small declines among older students in mathematics and science as well as decreased proficiency among all students in writing.[7]

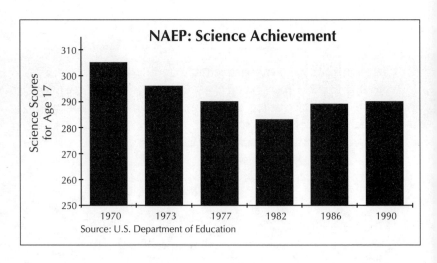

NAEP: Science Achievement

Science Scores for Age 17

Source: U.S. Department of Education

❏ While educational achievement has dropped, grades in American high schools have actually increased. In 1966, twice as many Cs as As were handed out. By 1978, the As exceeded the Cs. And by 1990, more than 20 percent of all entering college freshmen averaged A minus or above. At private universities, 54 percent of entering freshmen had high school averages of A minus or above.[8]

Factual Overview: High School Dropouts

❑ The dropout rate has fallen over the last decade. In 1972, the annual event dropout rate was over 6 percent.* By 1991, the rate was 4 percent. The decline in the dropout rate over the last decade occurred at each grade level and at each age. This decline is also evident in the dropout rates for white and black students.[9]

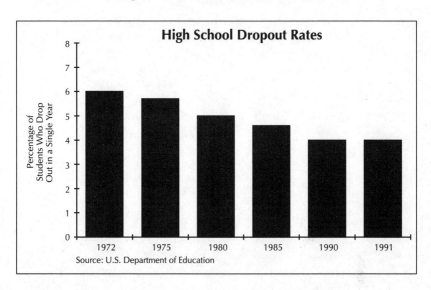

High School Dropout Rates

Source: U.S. Department of Education

❑ In 1991, some 4 percent of 15- to 24-year-olds in grades 10 to 12 dropped out of school—this represents approximately 348,000 students dropping out of school in 1991.[10]

*Event dropout rates measure the proportion of students who drop out in a single year without completing high school.

Factual Overview: Adult Literacy

❏ According to a study on adult literacy:[11]

❏ Twenty-one to 23 percent (40 to 44 million) of adults demonstrated skills in the lowest level of proficiency (25 percent of these people were immigrants, and two-thirds had ended their education before finishing high school), and 25 to 28 percent (50 million) of adults demonstrated skills in the second lowest level of proficiency.

❏ Yet, Americans feel good about poor performance: of the 40 to 44 million adults who demonstrated the most limited skills, only about 14 million of them said they did not read or write English well, and as few as 6 million of them said they get a lot of assistance with everyday prose, document, and quantitative literacy tasks.

❏ On each scale, 16 to 20 percent of adults with high school diplomas performed in the lowest level, and 33 to 38 percent performed in the second lowest level. Only 10 to 13 percent of high school graduates reached the two highest levels.

Commentary on Educational Achievement

❏ "And the greater the proportion of minds in any community which are educated, and [the] more thorough and complete the education which is given them, the more rapidly, through these sublime stages of progress, will that community advance in all the means of enjoyment and elevation; and the more it will outstrip and outshine its less educated neighbors."[12]

—HORACE MANN, 1848

❏ "If an unfriendly foreign power had attempted to impose on America the mediocre educational performance that exists today, we might well have viewed it as an act of war. As it stands, we have allowed this to happen to ourselves...we have, in effect, been committing an act of unthinking, unilateral educational disarmament."[13]

—National Commission on
Excellence in Education
A Nation at Risk, 1983

❏ "Large proportions, perhaps more than half, of our elementary, middle, and high-school students are unable to demonstrate competency in challenging subject matter in English, mathematics, science, history, and geography. Further, even fewer appear to be able to use their minds well."[14]

—National Assessment of
Educational Progress, 1990

❏ "Ninety-five percent of the kids who go to college in the United States would not be admitted to college anywhere else in the world."[15]

—ALBERT SHANKER
President, American Federation
of Teachers

❏ "Our schools today...tend to look upon disadvantaged minority students as though they were on the verge of a mental breakdown, to be protected from any undue stress.... Ideas like this are not just false. They are a kiss of death for minority youth and, if allowed to proliferate, will significantly stall the advancement of minorities."[16]

—JAIMIE ESCALANTE
Hiram Johnson High School

Spending

❑ *Total expenditures on public elementary and secondary education have increased more than 200 percent since 1960.*

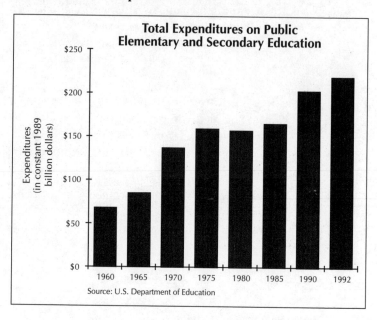

Total Expenditures on Public Elementary and Secondary Education

Source: U.S. Department of Education

Total Expenditures on Public Elementary and Secondary Education	
Year	Amount (billions of constant 1989 dollars)
1960	$ 67.5
1965	$ 83.2
1970	$136.8
1975	$159.0
1980	$157.0
1985	$164.5
1990	$205.3
1992	$216.8

Source: U.S. Department of Education

Factual Overview: Education Spending

❑ The United States spends more each year per student on public elementary and secondary education than Canada, Italy, West Germany, France, the United Kingdom, and Japan.[17]

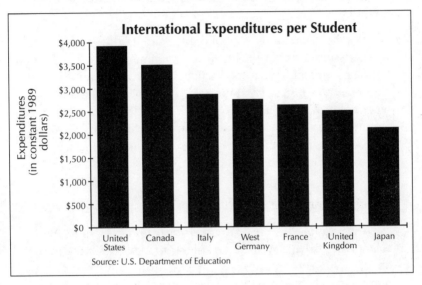

❑ Average teacher salaries, in constant dollars, have increased more than 25 percent since 1960.[18]

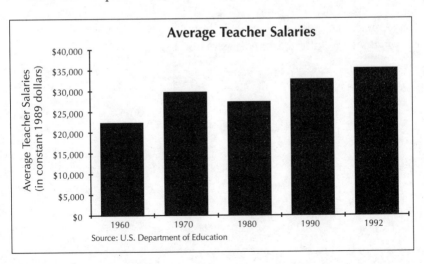

❏ The average teaching work year lasts 180 days, three-quarters of the 240-day year worked by the typical American with a full-time job. Compensated at the same daily rate for a forty-eight-week year, the average public school teacher would have earned $44,400 in 1991.[19]

❏ A smaller share of the school dollar is now being spent on student classroom instruction than at any time in recent history.[20] Between 1960 and 1984, local school spending on administration and other non-instructional functions grew by 107 percent in real terms, almost twice the rate of per pupil instructional expenses. During those same years, money spent on teacher salaries dropped from over 56 percent to under 41 percent of total elementary and secondary school spending.[21]

Commentary on Education Spending

❏ "The relationship between educational resources and measurable intellectual achievement is, at best, modest. Often the impact on what students actually learn seems small, debatable, or even nonexistent; here, America provides the most poignant example. Though we rank first on measures of resources and resource allocation, we are currently not first on any measures of intellectual achievement. This appears to be true whether we compare American students with their counterparts in other developed nations, or with their predecessors in this country."[22]

—BARBARA LERNER
Lerner Associates

❏ "Since the mid-Sixties there have been around 200 studies looking at the relationship between the inputs to schools, the resources spent on schools, and the performance of students. These studies tell a consistent and rather dramatic story. . . . Result 1 is that there is no systematic relationship between expenditures on schools and student performance. Result 2 is that there is no systematic relationship between the major ingredients of instructional expenditures per student—chiefly teacher education and teacher experience, which informally drive teacher salaries, and class size—and student performance."[23]

—ERIC HANUSHEK
University of Rochester

❏ "Education must increase its 'productivity'; we must get more education for the dollar. Not just to squeeze more out of the system—although that is not unimportant—but to demonstrate that good education is worth paying for. Business leaders know that these two ideas are related; unfortunately, educators do not. The public will support 'productive' education willingly; it is reluctant to support unproductive education."[24]

—DAVID KEARNS
Chairman, Xerox Corporation

Public Schools

❏ *Classroom teachers as a percentage of full-time school staff have dropped significantly during the past twenty years while the percentage of non-teaching staff has significantly increased.*

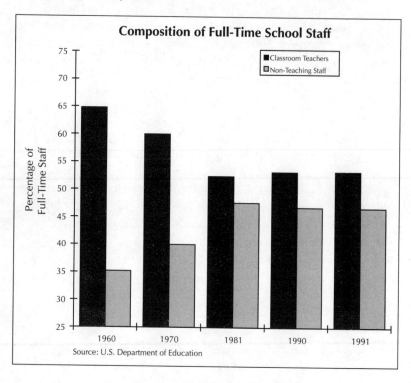

Composition of Full-Time School Staff

Source: U.S. Department of Education

Percentage of Full-Time School Staff

Year	Classroom Teachers	Non-Teaching Staff
1960	64.8	35.2
1970	60.0	40.0
1981	52.4	47.6
1990	53.2	46.8
1991	53.3	46.7

Source: U.S. Department of Education

❏ Over the last thirty years, the ratio of pupils to teachers has dropped in all 50 states and the District of Columbia, from a national average of 25.8 to 1 in 1960 to 17.2 to 1 in 1991.

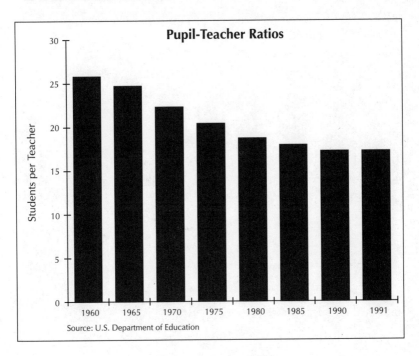

Pupil-Teacher Ratios

Students per Teacher

Source: U.S. Department of Education

Pupil-Teacher Ratios	
Year	Students per Teacher
1960	25.8
1965	24.7
1970	22.3
1975	20.4
1980	18.7
1985	17.9
1990	17.2
1991	17.2

Source: U.S. Department of Education

❑ *Since 1960, the average number of pupils per class has decreased in both elementary and secondary schools.*

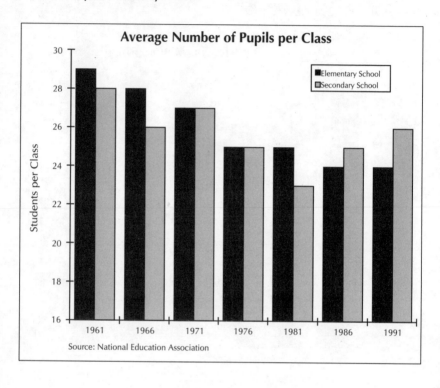

Average Number of Pupils per Class

Source: National Education Association

Average Number of Pupils per Class		
Year	Pupils per Class (elementary)	Pupils per Class (secondary)
1961	29	28
1966	28	26
1971	27	27
1976	25	25
1981	25	23
1986	24	25
1991	24	26

Source: National Education Association

Factual Overview: Enrollment

❑ Nationally, enrollment in the 1992–1993 school year was 7 percent below the 1972–1973 level and only about 13 percent above the 1959–1960 level.[25]

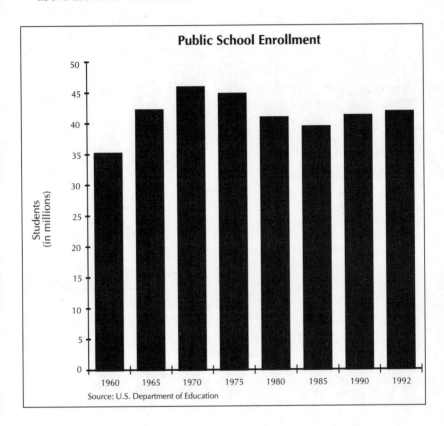

Public School Enrollment

Source: U.S. Department of Education

❑ There are more than 3 million schoolteachers in the United States—more than all the doctors, lawyers, and engineers combined.[26]

❑ From 1960 to 1984 the number of non-classroom instructional personnel in America's school systems grew 400 percent, nearly seven times the rate of growth in the number of classroom teachers. By 1987, full-time classroom teachers represented barely half

(53 percent) of all local school employment, with administrators representing 12 percent.[27]

Commentary on Public Schools

❏ "All Americans... would benefit from an education system that produced informed citizens. Education isn't just a service we obtain for our own daughters and sons and grandchildren. It is a public good, after defense perhaps our most important form of common provision and, in a sense, itself a defense against the ills that plague us at home. It has incalculable influence on the quality of social relationships, the vitality of our culture, the strength of our economy, the comfort we feel in our communities, and the wisdom of our government decisions. The better our education system, the better our public and private lives become."[28]

—CHESTER FINN
Vanderbilt University

❏ "I think somewhere down the line the curriculum changed. Things such as simple writing, spelling skills aren't emphasized anymore. Putting more focus on standardized testing does no good when kids don't know how to write. When a young person goes to fill out an application, they don't know how to do it. Even computer technology may be taking away the very thing they need to survive—writing skills. I don't see the spelling books anymore; I don't see the writing books."[29]

—VALERIE KING MARTIN
Former President, Atlanta Council
of PTAs

❏ "Historically, one of the most important ways for immigrant children to achieve economic, social, and political access to the American dream has been through education.... Now this critical avenue to success is being narrowed. The modern immigrant has been betrayed by a confederation of power-seeking politicians, unprincipled educators, and unwitting Americans."[30]

—ROBERT ROSSIER
National Advisory and
Coordinating Council on
Bilingual Education

Chapter 5

Popular Culture and Religion

Television

❏ In 1960, *the average daily television viewing per household was* 5:06 *hours. By* 1992, *it had increased to* 7:04 *hours.*

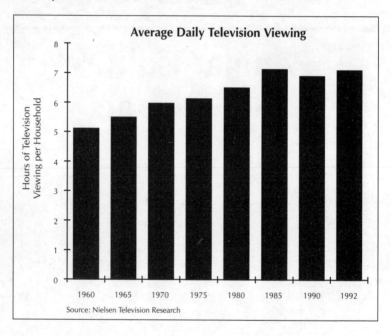

Average Daily Television Viewing

Source: Nielsen Television Research

Average Daily Television Viewing (per household)	
Year	Average hours per day
1960	5:06
1965	5:29
1970	5:56
1975	6:07
1980	6:36
1985	7:07
1990	6:55
1992	7:04

Source: Nielsen Television Research

Factual Overview: Television Viewing

❏ In 1990, more than 98 percent of all households had at least one television set.[1] More American households have televisions than have indoor plumbing.[2]

❏ The American average preschool child watches more than 27 hours of television per week, or about 4 hours per day.[3]

❏ The average teenager spends 1.8 hours per week reading, 5.6 hours per week on homework, and an average of 21 hours per week watching television, or about 3 hours per day.[4]

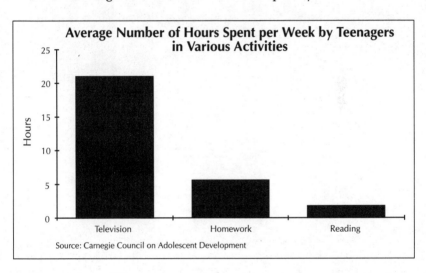

Average Number of Hours Spent per Week by Teenagers in Various Activities

Source: Carnegie Council on Adolescent Development

❏ In contrast to the 3 hours per day they spend watching TV, teenagers spend an average of 5 minutes per day alone with their fathers, and 20 minutes with their mothers. A Carnegie Corporation study found that even the time teenagers spend with their families consists primarily of eating or watching television together.[5]

❏ A 1991 survey revealed that only 2 percent of respondents think that television should have the greatest influence on children's values, but 56 percent believe that it does have the greatest influence—more than parents, teachers, and religious leaders combined.[6]

Factual Overview: Content of Television

❏ In the prime afternoon and evening hours the three largest networks broadcast a total of more than 65,000 sexual references each year. The average American now watches 14,000 references to sex in the course of a year.[7]

❏ The average child watches up to 8,000 made-for-TV murders and 100,000 acts of violence by the end of grade school.[8]

❏ Between 6 A.M. and midnight on April 2, 1992, ABC, CBS, NBC, PBS, USA, MTV, HBO, Fox, Turner, and WDCA-Washington combined aired the following:[9]

Act	Number of Scenes	Percentage of Total
Serious assaults (without guns)	389	20
Gunplay	362	18
Isolated punches	273	14
Pushing, dragging	272	14
Menacing threat with a weapon	226	11
Slaps	128	6
Deliberate destruction of property	95	5
Simple assault	73	4
All other types of violence	28	1

Source: Center for Media and Public Affairs

❏ *USA Today* watched one week of prime-time television on ABC, NBC, CBS, and Fox and found little similarity between the portrayal of life on television and the reality of life in 1993 America. Among the findings:[10]

❑ Of the 45 sex scenes shown on network television, 23 were of unmarried heterosexual couples, 16 were adulterous, 4 were between married heterosexuals, 1 involved a homosexual couple, and 1 involved unmarried, heterosexual teens.

❑ Among the 94 shows watched, 48 showed at least one violent act. All told there were 276 acts of violence in which 57 people were killed and 99 people were assaulted.

❑ Although 60 percent of Americans "never doubt the existence of God" and 42 percent attend church once a week, only 5 percent of TV characters practice any religion in any form.

Commentary on Television: National Commissions

❑ "[W]hen television is bad, nothing is worse. I invite you to sit down in front of your television set when your station goes on the air and stay there without a book, magazine, newspaper, profit-and-loss sheet, or rating book to distract you—and keep your eyes glued to that set until the station signs off. I can assure you that you will observe a vast wasteland. You will see a procession of game shows, violence, audience participation shows, formula comedies about totally unbelievable families, blood and thunder, mayhem, violence, sadism, murder, western badmen, western good men, private eyes, gangsters, more violence, and cartoons. And endlessly, commercials—many screaming, cajoling, and offending. And most of all, boredom. True, you will see a few things you will enjoy. But they will be very, very few. And if you think I exaggerate, try it."[11]

—NEWTON MINOW
Chairman, Federal
Communications Commission,
1961

❑ "We are deeply troubled by the television's constant portrayal of violence . . . in pandering to a public preoccupation with violence that television itself has helped to generate."[12]

—The Milton Eisenhower
Commission, 1969

❏ "Pervasive images of crime, violence and sexuality expose children and youth to situations and problems that often conflict with the common values of our society. . . . Accordingly, we call upon the media, especially television, to discipline themselves so that they are a part of the solution to our society's serious problems rather than a cause."[13]

—National Commission on
Children, 1992

Commentary on Television

❏ "The lowest-common-denominator quality of much of what appears on television and in other forms of popular culture—the constant barrage of violence and explicit sexuality—reinforces the loosening of human bonds, undermining the evolution of a mature person. For many people, it is affecting not just what they think about but also how they think, because it reinforces a kind of episodic, reactive, almost frantic mode of behavior. I think, on both the actual substance of entertainment and the process by which it's delivered, there are grounds to worry about its impact—particularly on children."[14]

—HILLARY RODHAM CLINTON
First Lady

❏ "Television violence affects youngsters of all ages, of both genders, at all socio-economic levels and all levels of intelligence. The effect is not limited to children already disposed to being aggressive and is not restricted to this country. . . . If media violence is reduced, the level of interpersonal aggression in our society will be reduced eventually."[15]

—LEONARD ERON
American Psychological
Association

Movies

❏ *Overall movie attendance in the United States is at its lowest point since 1980.*

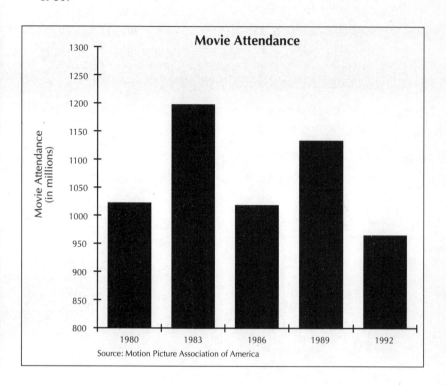

Movie Attendance

Source: Motion Picture Association of America

Movie Attendance	
Year	Admissions (millions)
1980	1,021.5
1983	1,196.9
1986	1,017.2
1989	1,132.5
1992	964.2

SOURCE: Motion Picture Association of America

Factual Overview: Movies

❏ According to a survey done by MTV and Yankelovich Partners, the United States is seen as the world's leading force in movies, music, and popular culture.[16]

❏ Preliminary estimates indicate that 1993 movie attendance will be significantly higher than 1992 figures.[17] This increase is at least partially due to the dramatically increased percentage of PG movies and the smaller percentage of R-rated films.[18]

❏ Despite an overall decrease in movie attendance, box office revenues have increased due to higher ticket prices:[19]

Year	Revenue (in billions)
1980	$2,748.5
1985	$3,749.4
1986	$3,778.0
1987	$4,252.9
1988	$4,458.4
1989	$5,033.4
1990	$5,021.8
1991	$4,803.2
1992	$4,871.1

Source: *Screen Digest*

❏ Taken together, the numbers since 1980 show that any given G or PG film is nearly five times more likely to place among the year's box office leaders than an R film.[20]

❏ Between 1980 and 1990, only 1 of the top 10 money-makers was rated R. Since 1983, there has not been a single year in which R movies did as well as PG or G films.[21]

❏ Despite the greater money-making potential of G, PG, and PG-13 films, in 1991, the Motion Picture Association of America estimated that 61 percent of all releases were rated R.[22]

❏ In a 1989 Media General/Associated Press poll of 1,804 people, 80 percent thought there was too much profanity in movies, 6 percent thought the profanity warranted, and the rest were undecided. Not one respondent thought there was too little.[23]

❏ In 1982, there were approximately 200 million videocassette rentals. In 1992, there were approximately 3.6 billion videocassette rentals.[24]

❏ The following are the approximate number of deaths recorded in five popular movies:[25]

Movie	Death Count
Die Hard 2	264
Rambo 3	106
The Wild Bunch	89
Robocop 2	74
Total Recall	74

Source: *The New York Times*

Commentary on Movies

❏ "Virtually every survey in recent years demonstrates a remarkably high level of dissatisfaction among Americans with motion pictures and with popular culture in general.... Why? What's the problem, is the camera out of focus?... No, my thesis is that most Americans dislike the movies because the values of the culture of Hollywood are out of focus. Hollywood has a dirty little secret: despite all the good news we hear about the box office grosses (which only reflect ticket prices that have risen at more than twice the rate of inflation), attendance at movie theaters in ... 1992 was the worst in 16 years."[26]

—MICHAEL MEDVED
author, *Hollywood vs. America*

❑ "Together, I think we can make the needed changes [to the motion picture industry]. If we don't, this decade will be noted in the history books as the embarrassing legacy of what began as a great art form. We will be labeled 'the decline of the empire'... any smart business person can see what we must do—make more 'PG'-rated films."[27]

—MARK CANTON
President, Universal Pictures

❑ "Movie violence is like eating salt. The more you eat, the more you need to eat to taste it at all. People are becoming immune to effects: the death counts have quadrupled, the blast power is increasing by the megaton, and they're becoming deaf to it. They've developed an insatiability for raw sensation."[28]

—ALAN K. PAKULA
Director, *All the President's Men* and
Presumed Innocent

Music

❏ **Since 1982, music unit* sales have increased more than 50 percent. In 1992, nearly 900 million units were sold.**

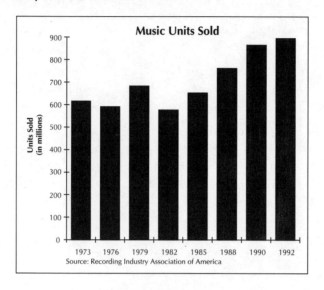

Music Units Sold

Year	Units (in millions)
1973	616.0
1976	591.6
1979	683.0
1982	577.4
1985	653.0
1988	761.9
1990	865.7
1992	895.5

SOURCE: Recording Industry Association of America

* Music units include CDs, CD singles, cassettes, cassette singles, LPs/EPs, vinyl singles, and music videos.

Factual Overview: Music

❏ Rock music leads the music market with about 33 percent of all consumer purchases, down from about 50 percent of all purchases in 1982. Country music is the fastest growing genre in sales.[29]

❏ Fifteen- to nineteen-year-olds buy more music than any other monitored age group.[30]

❏ Between the seventh and twelfth grades, the average teenager listens to 10,500 hours of rock music, just slightly less than the entire number of hours spent in the classroom from kindergarten through high school.[31]

❏ On the popular 2-Live Crew album *Nasty as They Wanna Be* (which sold 1.7 million copies), there are 226 uses of the word "fuck," 81 uses of the word "shit," 163 uses of the word "bitch," 87 descriptions of oral sex, and 117 explicit terms for male or female genitalia.[32]

Commentary on Music

❏ "[M]usical training is a more potent instrument than any other, because rhythm and harmony find their way into the inward places of the soul, on which they mightily fasten, imparting grace."[33]

—PLATO
The Republic

❏ "Over the past decade the messages portrayed by certain types of rock music...may well present a real threat to the physical health and well-being of especially vulnerable children and adolescents....Lyrics promoting drug and alcohol use, sexual exploitation, bigotry, and racism are combined with rhythms and intensities that appeal to youth. Physicians should know about [these] potentially destructive themes....Members of the entertainment industry...should exercise greater responsibility in presenting such music to young people."[34]

—Council on Scientific Affairs,
American Medical Association

❏ Rebuttal to charge that opponents of rap are racists: "We [the NAACP] are particularly offended by their [obscene rappers'] efforts to wrap the mantle of the black cultural experience around their performances by saying this is the way it is in the black community, and that they are authentic purveyors of our heritage. Our cultural experience does not include debasing our women, the glorification of violence, the promotion of deviant sexual behavior, or the tearing into shreds of our cherished mores and standards of behavior."[35]

—BENJAMIN HOOKS
NAACP

Commentary on Popular Culture

❏ "Broadcasting, to serve the public interest, must have a soul and a conscience, a burning desire to excel, as well as to sell; the urge to build the character, citizenship, and intellectual stature of people, as well as to expand the gross national product.... By no means do I imply that broadcasters disregard the public interest.... But a much better job can be done, and should be done."[36]

—Governor LEROY COLLINS
President, National Association of
Broadcasters, 1961

❏ "Today's mass culture would not know an idea, subversive or otherwise, if it met one. It traffics instead in sensibility and image, with a premium on the degrading: rap lyrics in which women are for using and abusing, movies in which violence is administered with a smirk and smile. Jack Nicholson's much celebrated Joker in *Batman*—acid in the face with a laugh—is about as close as one gets to cultural evil. Casual cruelty, knowing sex. Nothing could be better designed to rob youth of its most ephemeral gift: innocence. The ultimate effect of our mass culture is to make children older than their years, to turn them into the knowing, cynical pseudo-adult that is by now the model kid of the TV sitcom. It is a crime against children to make them older than their years. And it won't do for the purveyors of cynicism to hide behind the First Amendment. Of course they have the right to publish Ice-T and peddle *Batman* to kids. But they should have the decency not to."[37]

—CHARLES KRAUTHAMMER
Syndicated Columnist

Church Membership

❏ Since 1960, church and synagogue membership has increased almost 30 percent, although as a percentage of population, church and synagogue membership is slightly lower now than in 1960.

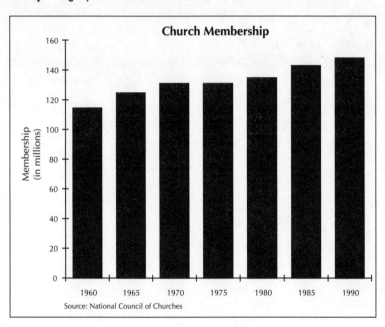

Church Membership

Membership (in millions)

Source: National Council of Churches

Year	Members (in millions)	Membership as a Percentage of Population	Sunday School (in millions)
1960	114.4	63.3	43.2
1965	124.7	64.2	46.9
1970	131.0	63.8	41.1
1975	131.0	60.6	35.4
1980	134.8	59.2	33.5
1985	142.9	59.9	29.7
1990	148.1	59.3	28.4

Source: National Council of Churches

Factual Overview: Church Membership

❏ America's mainline Protestant churches (Methodist, Presbyterian, Congregationalist, and Episcopal) have lost between one-fifth and one-third of the membership that they claimed in 1965, and the proportion of the population of Americans affiliated with them has reached a twentieth-century low.[38]

❏ Meanwhile, "Biblically conservative" denominations and other conservative Christian fellowships are among the fastest growing churches. This is especially true in major metropolitan centers.[39]

❏ More than 85 percent of the country identifies itself as either Protestant or Catholic:[40]

Religious Affiliations	
Religion	Percent
Protestants	59
Catholics	27
Jews	2
Muslims	1
Eastern Orthodox	1
Others	3
None	7
SOURCE: Gallup	

❏ According to one study, only 20 percent of Protestants and 28 percent of Catholics attend church in any given week—much lower than previous estimates.[41]

❏ With all other factors being equal, inner-city residents who go to church are far less likely to commit a crime or use drugs or drop out of school and are more likely to hold a job.[42]

Commentary on Religion

❏ "Of all the dispositions and habits which lead to political prosperity, Religion and Morality are indispensable supports. In vain would that man claim the tribute of patriotism who should labor to subvert these great pillars of human happiness, these firmest props of the duties of men and citizens. . . . And let us with caution indulge the supposition that morality can be maintained without religion. Whatever may be conceded to the influence of refined education on minds of peculiar structure, reason and experience both forbid us to expect that national morality can prevail in exclusion of religious principle."[43]

—GEORGE WASHINGTON, 1796

❏ "While the church may seem to be experiencing a season of growth and prosperity, it is failing to move people to commitment and sacrifice. The hard truth is that we have substituted an institutionalized religion for the life-changing dynamic of a living faith. . . . When compared with previous generations of believers, we seem among the most thoroughly at peace with our culture, the least adept at transforming society, and the most desperate for a meaningful faith. Our *raison d'être* is confused, our mission obscured, and our existence as a people in jeopardy."[44]

—CHARLES COLSON
Prison Fellowship

❏ "There is little hope for democracy if the hearts of men and women in democratic societies cannot be touched by a call to something greater than themselves. Political structures, state institutions, collective ideals are not enough. We Parliamentarians can legislate for the rule of law. You the Church can teach the life of faith. When all is said and done, a politician's role is a humble one."[45]

—MARGARET THATCHER
Prime Minister of Great Britain,
1979–1990

Appendix

Social Spending and Economic Growth

Government social spending covers the functions of: direct income support, medical aid, housing, and other welfare assistance. Total social spending figures include transfer programs assisting the general population such as Social Security and Medicare, as well as conventional welfare programs targeted at low-income persons such as Food Stamps and Aid to Families with Dependent Children.

❏ Measured in constant 1990 dollars, total social spending by all levels of government rose from $143.73 billion to $787.0 billion between 1960 and 1990, more than a five-fold increase. As a percentage of the Gross National Product, spending rose from 6.73 in 1960 to 14.4 in 1990.

	Total Social Spending	
Year	Constant 1990 Dollars (in billions)	Percentage of GNP
1960	143.725	6.73
1965	187.998	6.96
1970	301.129	9.33
1975	479.839	13.03
1980	584.839	13.58
1985	683.254	13.93
1990	787.000	14.40

Source: U.S. Department of Health and Human Services

❏ Total means-tested welfare spending by federal, state, and local governments equaled $211.9 billion in 1990. This figure comprises $54.9 billion in cash aid; $97.5 billion in medical aid; $25.3 billion in food assistance; $24.3 billion in housing and energy aid; $6.3 billion in social services; and $3.6 billion in community development and urban aid.

Means-Tested Welfare Spending		
Year	Constant 1990 Dollars (in billions)	Percentage of GNP
1960	28.9	1.4
1965	40.9	1.5
1970	77.0	2.4
1975	131.4	3.6
1980	159.3	3.7
1985	176.4	3.6
1990	211.9	3.9

Source: U.S. Department of Health and Human Services

Measured in constant 1990 dollars, means-tested welfare spending rose from $28.9 billion in 1960 to $211.9 billion in 1990—a seven-fold increase. As a percentage of the GNP, spending rose from 1.4 in 1960 to 3.9 in 1990. Government welfare spending takes nearly the same share of the GNP now as it did during the Great Depression of the 1930s, when nearly a quarter of the work force was unemployed.

In contrast to general social spending programs, means-tested welfare programs provide assistance targeted at poor and low-income persons and economically depressed communities. Means-tested welfare spending figures thus exclude programs that provide transfers to the general population such as Social Security, unemployment insurance, and Medicare for the middle class. The federal government operates over 60 means-tested welfare programs providing: cash aid, medical aid, housing, food assistance, social services, and community development. These programs include Aid to Families with Dependent Children, Food Stamps, Medicaid, public housing, Supplemental Security Income, and many others.

❏ The family tax rate rose from 4 percent of income in 1950, to 12 percent in 1960, and to 16 percent in 1970. This tax calculation includes federal income tax and both the employee and so-called employer share of Social Security tax. The tax bite on families was most severe during the 1970s. During that decade for every $1.00 in real income gained (above the rate of inflation) federal taxes took 66 cents. The 1980s was the only decade in the postwar period in which federal taxes on families with children did not increase. The federal tax burden on the average family of four in 1990 was 24 percent, the same level as in 1980.

Federal Tax Burden on Families with Children	
Year	Percent of Income
1960	12
1965	14
1970	16
1975	18
1980	24
1985	24
1990	24

Source: The Heritage Foundation

❏ The amount of money Americans give to charities has more than tripled since 1960.

	Charitable Contributions	
Year	Constant 1990 dollars (in billions)	Charitable Contributions (as percentage of GNP)
1960	36.90	1.7
1965	46.74	1.7
1970	66.77	2.1
1975	65.89	1.8
1980	76.70	1.8
1985	98.14	2.0
1990	117.50	2.2

Source: Statistical Abstract of the U.S.

❏ The percentage of people owning homes has remained relatively steady since 1973.

Percentage of Population Owning Homes	
Year	Percentage
1973	64
1976	65
1980	66
1983	65
1987	64
1989	64

Source: U.S. Bureau of the Census

❏ American Gross Domestic Product has nearly tripled and per capita GDP has nearly doubled since 1960.

	GDP Growth	
Year	GDP (in billions of constant 1987 dollars)	Per Capita
1960	1,970.8	10,903
1965	2,470.5	12,712
1970	2,873.9	14,013
1975	3,221.7	14,917
1980	3,776.3	16,584
1985	4,279.8	17,944
1990	4,877.5	19,513
1991	4,821.0	19,077
1992 (preliminary)	4,919.9	19,210

Source: U.S. Department of Commerce

❏ About 9 of 10 Americans own their own car.

Percentage of Households Owning Automobiles	
Year	Percentage
1962	77
1969	79
1977	85
1983	87
1988	90

Source: *The First Universal Nation*, Ben Wattenberg

Source Notes

Government Printing Office is abbreviated as GPO throughout the source notes section.

Chapter 1: Crime

1. U.S. Department of Justice, Federal Bureau of Investigation, *Crime in the United States, 1992* (Washington, DC: GPO, 1993).

2. Ibid.

3. U.S. Department of Justice, Bureau of Justice Statistics, *Sourcebook of Criminal Justice Statistics, 1992* (Washington, DC: GPO, 1993).

4. U.S. Department of Justice, Bureau of Justice Statistics, "Lifetime Likelihood of Victimization," 1987.

5. Clinton Rossiter, ed., *The Federalist Papers* (New York: Mentor, 1961).

6. Cited in Ed Kilgore, "Safer Streets and Neighborhoods," *Mandate for Change* (New York: Berkley Books, 1993).

7. Cited in Daniel Patrick Moynihan, "Toward a New Intolerance," *The Public Interest*, Summer 1993.

8. James K. Stewart, "The Urban Strangler," *Policy Review*, Summer 1986.

9. James Q. Wilson and Richard Herrnstein, *Crime and Human Nature* (New York: Simon & Schuster, 1986).

10. U.S. Department of Justice, Bureau of Justice Statistics, "Lifetime Likelihood of Victimization," 1987.

11. U.S. Department of Justice, Bureau of Justice Statistics, "International Crime Rates," May 1988.

12. U.S. Department of Justice, Federal Bureau of Investigation, *Crime in the United States, 1992* (Washington, DC: GPO 1993.)

13. U.S. Department of Justice, Bureau of Justice Statistics, *Sourcebook of Criminal Justice Statistics*, 1992 (Washington, DC: GPO, 1993); Mark Hoffman, ed., *The World Almanac and Book of Facts*, 1993 (New York: Pharos Books, 1993).

14. New York Police Department, Crime Analysis Unit, found in Daniel Patrick Moynihan, "Toward a New Intolerance," *The Public Interest*, Summer 1993.

15. Morton Kondracke, "Crime on the Political Backburner?" *The Washington Times*, December 14, 1992.

16. John J. DiIulio, Jr., "A Limited War on Crime That We Can Win: Two Lost Wars Later," *Brookings Review*, Fall 1992.

17. U.S. Department of Justice, *Criminal Victimization in the United States, 1990*, cited in Ed Kilgore, "Safer Streets and Neighborhoods," *Mandate for Change*, 1993.

18. John J. DiIulio, Jr., "Community Policing: Can It Cut Crime?" Wisconsin Policy Research Institute, November 1993.

19. Morgan Reynolds, "Myths about Gun Control," National Center for Policy Analysis, December 1992.

20. U.S. Department of Justice, Bureau of Justice Statistics, *Sourcebook of Criminal Justice Statistics*, 1992 (Washington, DC: GPO, 1993).

21. C. Everett Koop and George Lundberg, "Violence in America: A Public Health Emergency: Time to Bite the Bullet Back," *Journal of the American Medical Association*, June 10, 1992.

22. U.S. Department of Justice, Bureau of Alcohol, Tobacco and Firearms study, cited in Jeffrey Snyder, "A Nation of Cowards," *The Public Interest*, Fall 1993.

23. Gary Kleck, Florida State University criminologist, cited in ibid.

24. Morgan Reynolds, "Why Does Crime Pay?" National Center for Policy Analysis, December 8, 1992.

25. Unpublished tabulations, U.S. National Center for Health Statistics, National Vital Statistics System, in Karl Zinsmeister, *Breakdown: How America's Fraying Family Ties Threaten Our Future*, 1995 (forthcoming).

26. Richard Riordan, *Turning LA Around*, 1993.

27. American Psychological Association, *Violence and Youth*, 1993.

28. U.S. Department of Justice, Federal Bureau of Investigation, *Crime in*

the United States, 1992, cited in Jill Smolowe, "Danger in the Safety Zone," Time, August 23, 1993.

29. George Gilder, Men and Marriage (Gretna, LA: Pelicon Publishing, 1986).

30. Marvin Wolfgang, University of Pennsylvania, cited in Eugene Methvin, "An Anti-Crime Solution: Lock Up More Criminals," The Washington Post, January 15, 1992.

31. U.S. Department of Justice, Project Triggerlock: Incarcerating the Armed Criminal, 1992.

32. U.S. Department of Justice, Bureau of Justice Statistics, Sourcebook of Criminal Justice Statistics, 1992 (Washington, DC: GPO, 1993).

33. Ibid.

34. Colin McCord and Harold Freeman, "Excess Mortality in Harlem," The New England Journal of Medicine, January 1990.

35. U.S. Department of Justice, Bureau of Justice Statistics, Sourcebook of Criminal Justice Statistics, 1992 (Washington, DC: GPO, 1993).

36. U.S. Department of Justice, Office of Policy Development, The Case for More Incarceration, 1992.

37. U.S. Department of Justice, Bureau of Justice Statistics, Sourcebook of Criminal Justice Statistics, 1992 (Washington, DC: GPO, 1993).

38. Daniel Patrick Moynihan, "Defining Deviancy Down," The American Scholar, Winter 1993.

39. John J. DiIulio, Jr., "The Value of Prisons," The Wall Street Journal, May 13, 1992.

40. David Rubinstein, "Don't Blame Crime on Joblessness," The Wall Street Journal, November 13, 1992.

41. Adam Walinsky, "What It's Like to Be in Hell," The New York Times, December 4, 1987.

42. U.S. Department of Justice, Office of the Attorney General, Combating Violent Crime, 1992.

43. U.S. Department of Justice, Bureau of Justice Statistics, Sourcebook of Criminal Justice Statistics, 1992 (Washington, DC: GPO, 1993).

44. Nancy Lewis, "Delinquent Girls Take a Turn," The Washington Post, December 23, 1992; "The Young and the Violent," The Wall Street Journal, September 23, 1992.

45. Daniel Goleman, "Hope Seen for Curbing Youth Violence," *The New York Times*, August 13, 1993.

46. U.S. Department of Education, cited in Mary Jordan, "Summit Searches for Cease-Fire in Violence Enveloping Children," *The Washington Post*, July 22, 1993.

47. Ibid.

48. U.S. Department of Justice, Bureau of Justice Statistics, *Sourcebook of Criminal Justice Statistics, 1992* (Washington, DC: GPO, 1993).

49. U.S. Department of Justice, Federal Bureau of Investigation, *Crime in the United States, 1992* (Washington, DC: GPO, 1993).

50. Philip Lawler, "The New Counterculture," *The Wall Street Journal*, August 13, 1993.

51. Joseph Perkins, "The Young and Violent," *The Washington Times*, September 11, 1992.

52. "Bad Boys," *The Wall Street Journal*, September 28, 1993.

53. Karl Zinsmeister, "Growing Up Scared," *The Atlantic Monthly*, June 1990.

54. U.S. Department of Justice, Bureau of Justice Statistics, cited in John J. DiIulio, Jr., "The Value of Prisons," *The Wall Street Journal*, May 13, 1992.

55. Ibid.

56. U.S. Department of Justice, Federal Bureau of Investigation, cited in Jerry Seper, "Bush Justice Officials Form Anti-Crime Group," *The Washington Times*, October 24, 1993.

57. Alfred Kazin, "What's Wrong with America," *Forbes*, September 1992.

58. U.S. Department of Justice, Federal Bureau of Investigation, *Crime in the United States, 1992* (Washington, DC: GPO, 1993).

59. Morgan Reynolds, "Why Does Crime Pay?" National Center for Policy Analysis, December 8, 1992.

60. Charles Colson and David Van Ness, *Convicted: New Hope for Ending America's Crime Crisis*, 1989.

61. U.S. Department of Justice, Bureau of Justice Statistics, *Sourcebook of Criminal Justice Statistics, 1992* (Washington, DC: GPO, 1993).

62. U.S. Department of Justice, cited in Charles David Rothenberg, "Felons, Freedom and Fear," *Los Angeles Times*, January 24, 1990.

63. U.S. Department of Justice, Office of Policy Development, *The Case for More Incarceration*, 1992.

64. John J. DiIulio, Jr., "America's Ticking Crime Bomb: Can It Be Defused," *Wisconsin Interest*, Spring 1994 (forthcoming).

65. Cited in Cindy Hall, "Martin Luther King, Jr.: 'Riots Are Voices of the Unheard,' Gannet News Service, May 8, 1992.

66. John J. DiIulio, Jr., "The Crime of Not Punishing: A History of U.S. Justice," *The Washington Times*, September 12, 1993.

67. Gordon Tullock, "Does Punishment Deter Crime?" *The Public Interest*, Fall 1974.

68. Stanley Brubaker, "In Praise of Punishment," *The Public Interest*, Fall 1989.

69. Terence Pell and John Walters, "What Did We Do in the Drug War? Plenty," *The Washington Post*, April 16, 1993.

70. The White House, Office of National Drug Control Policy, *National Drug Control Strategy*, 1992.

71. The White House, Office of National Drug Control Policy, *Breaking the Cycle of Drug Abuse: 1993 Interim National Drug Control Strategy*.

72. The White House, Office of National Drug Control Policy, *National Drug Control Strategy*, 1992.

73. Ibid.

74. Children's Defense Fund, *The Adolescent and Young Adult Fact Book*, 1992.

75. U.S. Congress, House of Representatives, Select Committee on Children, Youth, and Families, *A Decade of Denial: Teens and AIDS in America*, 1992.

76. Cited in George Will, "How Reagan Changed America," *Newsweek*, January 9, 1989.

77. Cited in Karl Zinsmeister, "Growing Up Scared," *The Atlantic*, June 1990.

Chapter 2: Family and Children

1. U.S. Department of Commerce, Bureau of the Census, Current Population Reports, Series P-20, No. 458, 1991.

2. U.S. Department of Commerce, Bureau of the Census, Current Population Reports, Series P-60, No. 174, *Money Income in Households, Families, and Persons in the United States*, 1990.

3. U.S. Department of Commerce, Bureau of the Census, Current Population Reports, Series P-20, *Marital Status and Living Arrangements*, annual.

4. U.S. Department of Commerce, Bureau of the Census, Current Population Reports, Series P-25, No. 1018, *Projections of the Population of the United States, by Age, Sex and Race: 1988-2080*, 1989.

5. U.S. Department of Health and Human Services, National Center for Health Statistics, *Vital Statistics of the United States, 1989*, vol. 1, *Natality*.

6. U.S. Department of Commerce, Bureau of the Census, *Statistical Abstract of the United States, 1992* (Washington, DC: GPO, 1993); Victor R. Fuchs and Diane M. Reklis, "America's Children: Economic Perspectives and Policy Options," *Science*, January 3, 1992.

7. President Lyndon B. Johnson, Howard University Commencement, June 1965, in *Families First*, National Commission on America's Urban Families, 1993.

8. Karl Zinsmeister, "Raising Hiroko," *The American Enterprise*, March/April 1990.

9. Daniel Yankelovich, "Foreign Policy After the Election," *Foreign Affairs*, Fall 1992.

10. U.S. Department of Health and Human Services, *Vital Statistics of the United States, 1991* (forthcoming) vol. 1, *Natality* (Washington, DC: GPO, 1993).

11. Congressional testimony of Lee Rainwater, Harvard University, in George Will, "The Tragedy of Illegitimacy," *The Washington Post*, October 31, 1993.

12. Nicholas Eberstadt, "A Revolution in 'Family' That Is Eating Its Children," *The Washington Times*, September 24, 1993.

13. U.S. Department of Commerce, Bureau of the Census, Current Population Reports, Population Characteristics, Series P-20, No. 470, "Fertility of American Women: 1992."

14. U.S. Department of Health and Human Services, *Vital Statistics of the United States, 1991* (forthcoming), vol. 1, *Natality* (Washington, DC: GPO, 1993).

15. Charles Murray, "The Coming White Underclass," *The Wall Street Journal*, October 29, 1993.

16. Michael Novak, "Families: The Best Anti-Poverty Plan," *The Washington Times*, February 5, 1993.

17. Cited in William Bennett, *The De-Valuing of America* (New York: Simon & Schuster, 1992).

18. Barbara Dafoe Whitehead, "Dan Quayle Was Right," *The Atlantic Monthly*, April 1993.

19. David Blankenhorn, David Popenoe, and Barbara Dafoe Whitehead, *Fatherless America*, 1994 (forthcoming).

20. U.S. Department of Commerce, Bureau of the Census, *Current Population Reports*, "Marital Status and Living Arrangement," Series P-20, No. 461, 1992.

21. U.S. Department of Commerce, Bureau of the Census, *Statistical Abstract of the United States, 1992* (Washington, DC: GPO 1993).

22. Daniel Patrick Moynihan, "Toward a Post-Industrial Social Policy," *The Public Interest*, Summer 1989.

23. National Center for Health Statistics, *Survey on Child Health*, 1988.

24. Nicholas Zill, Donna Morrison, and Mary Jo Coiro, "Long-Term Effects of Parental Divorce on Parent-Child Relationships, Adjustment, and Achievement in Young Adulthood," *Journal of Family Psychology*, 1993.

25. Barbara Dafoe Whitehead, "Dan Quayle Was Right," *The Atlantic Monthly*, April 1993.

26. Ibid.

27. U.S. Department of Commerce, Bureau of the Census, *Current Population Reports*, "Money Income of Households, Families, and Persons: 1991," Series P-60, No. 180, 1992.

28. Cited in Ralph Reed, "Casting a Wider Net," *Policy Review*, Summer 1993.

29. David Popenoe, "The Controversial Truth," *The New York Times*, December 26, 1992.

30. Christopher Jencks, "Review: The Truly Disadvantaged," *The New Republic*, June 13, 1988.

31. William Galston and Elaine Kamarck, "A Progressive Family Policy for the 1990s," *Mandate for Change* (New York: Berkley Books, 1993).

32. U.S. Department of Commerce, Bureau of the Census, *Statistical Abstract of the United States, 1992* (Washington, DC: GPO, 1993).

33. Ibid.

34. Nicholas Davidson, "Life without Father: America's Greatest Social Catastrophe," *Policy Review*, Winter 1990.

35. James Q. Wilson, *The Moral Sense* (New York: The Free Press, 1993).

36. U.S. Department of Health and Human Services, National Center for Health Statistics, "Advance Report of Final Divorce Statistics 1988," *Monthly Vital Statistics Report 39*, 1991.

37. National Commission on Children, *Just the Facts: A Summary of Recent Information on America's Children and Their Families* (Washington, DC, 1993).

38. Barbara Dafoe Whitehead, "Dan Quayle Was Right," *The Atlantic Monthly*, April 1993.

39. Norval Glenn and Kathryn Kramer, University of Texas, cited in Barbara Kantrowitz, "Breaking the Divorce Cycle," *Newsweek*, January 13, 1992.

40. Amitai Etzioni, *The Spirit of Community: Rights, Responsibilities, and the Communitarian Agenda* (New York: Crown Publishers, 1993).

41. William Galston and Elaine Kamarck, "Putting Children First: A Progressive Family Policy for the 1990s," Progressive Policy Institute, 1992.

42. U.S. Department of Commerce, Bureau of the Census, *Statistical Abstract of the United States, 1992* (Washington, DC: GPO, 1993).

43. U.S. Department of Commerce, Bureau of the Census, *Current Population Reports*, Series P-60, No. 181, "Poverty in the United States, 1991," in National Commission on America's Urban Families, *Families First* (Washington, DC, 1993).

44. Ibid.

45. William Galston, "A Liberal-Democratic Case for the Two-Parent Family," *The Responsive Community*, Winter 1990/91.

46. U.S. Department of Commerce, Bureau of the Census, *Statistical Abstract of the United States, 1992* (Washington, DC: GPO, 1993).

47. William Galston and Elaine Kamarck, "A Progressive Family Policy for the 90s," in *Mandate for Change* (New York: Berkely Books, 1993).

48. National Commission on Children, *Beyond Rhetoric: A New American Agenda for Children and Families*, 1991 (Washington, DC, 1991).

49. U.S. Department of Commerce, Bureau of the Census, *Statistical Abstract of the United States, 1992* (Washington, DC: GPO, 1993).

50. Robert Rector, "A Comprehensive Urban Policy: How to Fix Welfare and Revitalize America's Inner Cities," The Heritage Foundation, 1993.

51. U.S. Bureau of the Census, cited in Douglas Besharov, "Poverty, Welfare Dependency, and the Underclass," University of California, Los Angeles, January 1993.

52. U.S. Bureau of the Census, cited in Daniel Patrick Moynihan, "The Children of the State: Welfare Reform, Congress and Family Responsibility," *The Washington Post*, November 25, 1990.

53. Ibid.

54. Ibid.

55. Robert Rector, "Perplexities of the Poverty Data," The Washington Times, September 8, 1992.

56. U.S. Department of Commerce, Bureau of the Census, Statistical Abstract of the United States, 1992 (Washington, DC: GPO, 1993).

57. Ibid.

58. Ibid.

59. Gertrude Himmelfarb, Poverty and Compassion: The Moral Imagination of the Late Victorians (New York: Knopf, 1991).

60. Myron Magnet, The Dream and the Nightmare (New York: William Morrow & Co., 1992).

61. Charles Murray, "The Legacy of the 60's," Commentary, July 1992.

62. "Abortion and a Nation at War," First Things, October 1992.

63. Stanley Henshaw, Lisa Koonin, and Jack Smith, "Characteristics of U.S. Women Having Abortions, 1987," Family Planning Perspectives, March/April 1991.

64. Ibid.

65. Ibid.

66. Ibid.

67. Morbidity and Mortality Weekly Report, "Abortion Surveillance," vol. 41, no. 50, December 18, 1992.

68. Aida Torres and Jacqueline Darroch Forrest, "Why Do Women Have Abortions?" Family Planning Perspectives, July/August 1988.

69. Bill Clinton, Address in Chillicothe, Ohio, February 1993.

70. Mary Ann Glendon, "U.S. Abortion Law: Still the Most Permissive on Earth," The Wall Street Journal, July 1, 1992.

71. James Davison Hunter, "What Americans Really Think about Abortion," First Things, July 1992.

Chapter 3: Youth: Pathologies and Behavior

1. Children's Defense Fund, The State of America's Children, 1992 (Washington: DC, 1992).

2. Kristin Moore, Nancy Snyder, Charles Halla, "Facts at a Glance," Child Trends, March 1993.

3. C. D. Hayes, ed., *Risking the Future: Adolescent Sexuality, Pregnancy, and Childbearing*, 1987.

4. Children's Defense Fund, *The Adolescent and Young Adult Fact Book* (Washington, DC: 1991).

5. "Parents! What You Must Know about Your Teenager's Sex Life," *Good Housekeeping*, June 1993.

6. S. K. Henshaw and J. Van Dort, "Teenage Abortion, Birth, and Pregnancy Statistics: An Update," *Family Planning Perspectives* 21, 1989.

7. Ibid.

8. Charles Donovan, "Teenage Pregnancy: National Policies at the Crossroads," Family Research Council, 1989.

9. Eunice Kennedy Shriver, "Rx for Teen Pregnancy," *The Washington Post*, March 19, 1987.

10. Kingsley Davis, National Institutes of Health Publication, No. 81-2077.

11. Deborah Anne Dawson, "The Effects of Sex Education on Adolescent Behavior," *Family Planning Perspectives*, 1986.

12. L. Douglas Wilder, "To Save the Black Family, The Young Must Abstain," *The Wall Street Journal*, 1991.

13. George Will, "The Disease of Violence," *The Washington Post*, November 29, 1992.

14. Edward Zigler, *Children: Developmental and Social Issues*, 1988; S. M. Finch and E. D. Poznaski, *Adolescent Suicide*, 1971; P. C. Hollinger, "Adolescent Suicide: An Epidemiological Study of Recent Trends," *American Journal of Psychiatry*, 1978.

Chapter 4: Education

1. Eric Hanushek, "The Economics of Schooling: Production and Efficiency in Public Schools," *Journal of Economic Literature*, September 1986.

2. Thomas Toch, Ted Gest, and Monika Guttman, "Violence in the Schools," *U.S. News & World Report*, November 8, 1993.

3. Gallup Organization, *Geography: An International Gallup Survey: Summary of Findings*. Study conducted for the National Geographic Society, 1988.

4. U.S. Department of Education, National Center for Education Statistics, International Assessment of Educational Progress, *A World of Differences*, 1989.

5. Ibid.

6. U.S. Department of Education, National Center for Education Statistics, National Assessment of Educational Progress, *1992 NAEP Trial State Assessment*, 1993.

7. U.S. Department of Education, National Center for Education Statistics, *The Condition of Education*, 1993 (Washington, DC: GPO, 1993).

8. Cooperative Institutional Research Program, *The American Freshman: National Norms for Fall 1989*, 1990.

9. U.S. Department of Education, National Center for Education Statistics, *Dropout Rates in the United States: 1991*.

10. Ibid.

11. U.S. Department of Education, Office of Educational Research and Improvement, *Adult Literacy in America*, September 1993.

12. Cited in Chester E. Finn, Jr., *We Must Take Charge* (New York: Free Press, 1991).

13. National Committee on Excellence in Education, *A Nation at Risk*, 1983.

14. Cited in Chester E. Finn, Jr., *We Must Take Charge* (New York: Free Press, 1991),

15. Cited in Carol Innerst, "Schools 'Really Bad' Says AFT Leader," *The Washington Times*, July 5, 1990.

16. Jaimie Escalante, "Hold to a Dream," *Network News and Views*, 1990.

17. U.S. Department of Education, National Center for Education Statistics, *The Condition of Education*, 1993 (Washington, DC: GPO, 1993).

18. U.S. Department of Education, National Center for Education Statistics, *Digest of Education Statistics*, 1992 (Washington, DC: GPO, 1992).

19. Chester E. Finn, Jr., *We Must Take Charge* (New York: Free Press, 1991).

20. U.S. Department of Education, Office of Planning, Budget and Evaluation, "Resource Allocations and Staffing Patterns in the Public Schools: 1959–60 to 1983–84," 1984.

21. U.S. Department of Education, *American Education: Making It Work*, 1988.

22. Barbara Lerner, "American Education: How Are We Doing?" *Public Interest*, Fall 1982.

23. Eric Hanushek, "How Business Can Save Education: A State Agenda for Reform," Heritage Foundation Conference, April 24, 1991.

24. Ibid.

25. U.S. Department of Education, cited in Empower America and the American Legislative Exchange Council, *The Report Card on American Education*, September 1993.

26. U.S. Department of Commerce, Bureau of the Census, *Statistical Abstract of the United States*, 1992 (Washington, DC: GPO, 1992).

27. U.S. Department of Education, National Center for Education Statistics, *The Condition of Education*, 1993.

28. Chester E. Finn, Jr., in John Murphy and Jeffry Schiller, *Tranforming America's Schools* (La Salle, IL: Open Court, 1992).

29. Barbara Kantrowitz, "A Nation Still at Risk," *Newsweek*, April 19, 1993.

30. Robert Rossier, "Training for the Ghetto," *Policy Review*, Summer 1983.

Chapter 5: Popular Culture and Religion

1. U.S. Department of Commerce, Bureau of the Census, *Statistical Abstract of the United States*, 1992 (Washington, DC: GPO, 1992).

2. James Twitchell, *Carnival Culture: The Trashing of Taste in America* (New York: Columbia University Press, 1992).

3. Brandon Centerwall, "Our Cultural Perplexities," *The Public Interest*, Spring 1993.

4. Carnegie Council on Adolescent Development, cited in Barbara Vobejda, "Home Alone, Glued to the TV," *The Washington Post*, December 10, 1992.

5. Ibid.

6. Mellman and Lazarus, 1991 *American Family Values Study: A Return to Family Values*, Mass Mutual American Family Values, 1991.

7. Louis Harris and Associates study, cited in Eleanor Blau, "Study Finds Barrage of Sex on TV," *The New York Times*, January 27, 1988.

8. American Psychological Association, cited in Marco della Cava, "Clean Up Your Act, Industry Told," *USA Today*, October 21, 1993.

9. Center for Media and Public Affairs, cited in Harry Waters, "Networks Under the Gun," *Newsweek*, July 12, 1993.

10. Barbara Hansen and Carol Knopes, "Prime Time Tuning Out Varied Culture," *USA Today*, July 6, 1993; Donna Gable, "In Search of Prime-Time Faith," *USA Today*, July 12, 1993.

11. Found in William Safire, *Lend Me Your Ears* (New York: Norton, 1992).

12. Cited in Harrison Rainie, Betsy Streisand, Monika Guttman, and Gordon Witkin, "Warning Shots at TV," *U.S. News & World Report*, July 12, 1993.

13. Cited in Charles Krauthammer, "Cultural Crimes against Children," *The Washington Post*, July 24, 1992.

14. Hillary Rodham Clinton, "I Worry about Television," *Parade*, April 11, 1993.

15. Dr. Leonard Eron, Testimony before the U. S. Senate Committee on Governmental Affairs, March 31, 1992.

16. Cited in "When It Comes to Pop Culture, We Are the World," *AdWeek*, November 2, 1991.

17. Steve Ginsberg, "Prehistoric Creatures May Lead the Way to Historic Box Office Showing," *Los Angeles Business Journal*, July 12, 1993.

18. Conversation with Michael Medved, November 8, 1993.

19. "Cinemas, Gross Box Office Revenue," *Screen Digest*, September 1992.

20. Michael Medved, *Hollywood vs. America* (New York: HarperCollins, 1992).

21. Ibid.

22. Ibid.

23. Cited in Michael Medved, "Hollwood's Dirty Little Secrets: Losing Money on Films America Hates," *Crisis*, March 1993.

24. The Video Software Dealers Association, "Video Industry Statistics, 1992."

25. Vincent Canby, "Now at a Theater Near You: A Skyrocketing Body Count," *The New York Times*, July 16, 1990.

26. Michael Medved, "Hollwood's Dirty Little Secrets: Losing Money on Films America Hates," *Crisis*, March 1993.

27. Mark Canton, Speech to Convention of Movie Exhibitors, March 9, 1993.

28. Cited in Tim Appelo, "Ultraviolence: Why Has This Been the Bloodiest Summer in Movie History?" *Entertainment Weekly*, August 1990.

29. Recording Industry Association of America, *The World Is Listening: 1992 Annual Report*.

30. Ibid.

31. Elizabeth Brown and William Hendee, "Adolescents and Their Music," *Journal of the American Medical Association*, September 22–29, 1989, vol. 262, no. 12.

32. Robert DeMoss, Jr., *Learn to Discern* (Grand Rapids, MI: Zondervan, 1992).

33. Plato, *The Republic* (New York: Vintage Classics, 1991).

34. Richard Harwood, "Is Television to Blame for Violence?" *Star Tribune*, April 22, 1993.

35. Michael Medved, "The New Sound of Music," *The Public Interest*, Fall 1992.

36. Found in William Safire, *Lend Me Your Ears* (New York: Norton, 1992).

37. Charles Krauthammer, "Cultural Crimes against Children," *The Washington Post*, July 24, 1992.

38. Benton Johnson, Dean Hoge, and Donald Luidens, "Mainline Churches: The Real Reason for Decline," *First Things*, March 1993.

39. Ibid.

40. Gallup poll, cited in Kenneth Woodward, "Dead End for the Mainline?" *Newsweek*, August 9, 1993.

41. Tom Roberts, "Report Says Church Attendance Is Half What Past Studies Claim," *The Washington Post*, September 4, 1993.

42. Karl Zinsmeister, *The Heritage Lectures*, No. 428, "Shaping America's Values Debate," September 15, 1992.

43. Found in William Safire, *Lend Me Your Ears* (New York: Norton, 1992).

44. Charles Colson, *The Body* (Dallas: Word, 1992).

45. Margaret Thatcher, "Address to the General Assembly of the Church of Scotland," *The Observer*, May 22, 1988.

WILLIAM J. BENNETT served as Director of the Office of National Drug Control Policy under President Bush and served as Secretary of Education and Chairman of the National Endowment for the Humanities under President Reagan. He has a bachelor of arts degree in philosophy from Williams College, a doctorate in political philosophy from the University of Texas, and a law degree from Harvard. Dr. Bennett is currently a co-director of Empower America, a Distinguished Fellow in Cultural Policy Studies at the Heritage Foundation, and a senior editor of *National Review* magazine. He, his wife, and two sons live in Chevy Chase, Maryland.